5-STEP CANINE CARE

You Don't Have to Be a Vet to Help Your Pet

Jet Parker

5-Step Canine Care © Copyright <<2020>> Jet Parker

All rights reserved. No part of this publication may be reproduced, distributed or transmitted in any form or by any means, including photocopying, recording, or other electronic or mechanical methods, without the prior written permission of the publisher, except in the case of brief quotations embodied in critical reviews and certain other noncommercial uses permitted by copyright law.

Although the author and publisher have made every effort to ensure that the information in this book was correct at press time, the author and publisher do not assume and hereby disclaim any liability to any party for any loss, damage, or disruption caused by errors or omissions, whether such errors or omissions result from negligence, accident, or any other cause.

Adherence to all applicable laws and regulations, including international, federal, state and local governing professional licensing, business practices, advertising, and all other aspects of doing business in the US, Canada or any other jurisdiction is the sole responsibility of the reader and consumer.

Neither the author nor the publisher assumes any responsibility or liability whatsoever on behalf of the consumer or reader of this material. Any perceived slight of any individual or organization is purely unintentional.

The resources in this book are provided for informational purposes only and should not be used to replace the specialized training and professional judgment of a health care or mental health care professional.

Neither the author nor the publisher can be held responsible for the use of the information provided within this book. Please always consult a trained professional before making any decision regarding treatment of yourself or others.

For more information, email info@creatureconcierge.com.

ISBN Ebook: 978-1-7353900-0-0
ISBN Paperback: 978-1-7353900-1-7

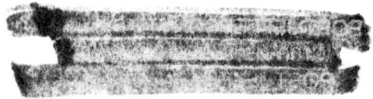

Get Your Free Gift!

FREE ESSENTIAL FORMS FOR

5-Story Canine Care

Plus Bonus Gift:

Greatest Doggie Distractions

To get the best experience with this book, download a set of the CANINE CARE GUIDE FORMS. These exclusive forms make it easier to implement the dog care practices you'll learn to improve your pet's health, happiness and life while lowering pet care costs too!

You can get a copy of all the CARE guide forms by visiting:
https://creatureconcierge.com/5-STEP_Canine_Care_BONUS_KIT.pdf

Dedication

To my parents, who taught me to love learning; to my dog clients, who taught me I could transform creature care. To the veterinarians and vet techs who graciously share their knowledge with me.

Table of Contents

Why You Want This Book ix

STEP ONE: PREPARATION 1

  1. Prepare! Prepare! Prepare! 3
  2. Prepare Your Pet's Medical Care Paperwork 5
  3. Prepare a First Aid Kit 15
  4. Prepare Your Emergency Skills 23
  5. Prepare for Disasters 27
  6. Prepare for Medical Expenses 33

STEP TWO: ATTENTION 39

  7. We've Got it All Wrong 41
  8. Pay Attention to Your Dog's Overall Health 43
  9. Pay Attention to Your Dog's Life Stage 49
  10. Pay Attention to Your Dog's Breed 59
  11. Pay Attention to Your Dog's Triggers 63
  12. Pay Attention to Your Dog's Red Flags 67
  13. Pay Attention to Your Dog's Treatments 73

STEP THREE: PREVENTION 83

  14. Why Didn't You Tell Me? 85
  15. Prevent Accidents At Home 87
  16. Prevent Accidents Outdoors 93
  17. Prevent Accidents Offsite 101
  18. Prevent Poisoning 111
  19. Prevent Dental Disease 121
  20. Prevent Obesity 125

STEP FOUR: NUTRITION 131

   21. The Big Three... 133

   22. A Mini Guide on Common Commercial Pet Foods 135

   23. Nutrition - For Health 143

STEP FIVE: EDUCATION 147

   24. Knowledge Unleashes Power 149

Why You Want This Book

At a time when science, research, and technology are at their finest, our pets' health and wellness are not. Too many dogs are overweight. Too many are plagued with chronic colitis, pancreatitis, obesity, diabetes, and cancer. Instead of living longer, healthier lives, the lifespan of pets today (as compared to fifty years ago) is shorter. Pet owners, devoted to these precious creatures, are often befuddled by simple dog care issues, overwhelmed by chronic health problems, confused by conflicting dog food information, and frustrated with expensive vet bills. Yet, pet owners' investment in their pets is cosmic. According to the American Pet Products Association (APPA), pet industry expenditures for 2019 were $95.7 billion. Most of this money went to pet food/treats ($36.9 billion), supplies/over the counter (OTC) medicine ($19.2 billion) and vet care/product sales ($29.3 billion).

When thinking over this conundrum, I had an epiphany. Everyone involved with the care of our dogs—veterinarians, groomers, daycare operators, dog walkers, trainers—are educated to excel at their jobs. Yet the dog owners, who spend more time with their pets than anyone else, receive virtually no training and education on canine care.

Realizing this, my mission for this book became clear: to equip pet owners with the fundamental knowledge, resources, and training to care effectively for their dogs. Instead of depending completely on veterinary practices designed to *reactively* solve problems regarding our dogs, why not train dog owners on how to *prevent* most of these problems?

Imagine what dog injuries could be eliminated, what tragic accidents avoided, what pet illnesses significantly reduced, and what money dog owners could save if they were better equipped to care proactively for their beloved creature kids. Whether you just got your first dog or you are enjoying the company of your fourth dog, I believe you will find this book immeasurably helpful.

This book, designed as a guide, is divided into five major areas of canine care: Preparation, Attention, Prevention, Nutrition, and Education.

Each section provides easy to follow tips, ideas, suppliers, experts, and must-have documents.

Collectively, this will empower you to ask smarter questions, to know what resources to access, and to understand what options you have regarding your dog's welfare. You will make more judicious decisions regarding your dog's health, wellness, diet, products, and activities and you will be better prepared for pet-related emergencies. The ultimate outcome: healthier dogs that live longer, higher-quality lives and parents that enjoy their company more while spending less on their care.

Step One

PREPARATION

CHAPTER 1

Prepare! Prepare! Prepare!

What are the odds? While finishing this segment of my book about preparing for pet emergencies and disasters, the world is experiencing a disaster of its own: the COVID-19 virus.

This worldwide pandemic literally changed our lives—and my businesses—overnight. This is especially true of Creature Concierge, my pet care company where both people and pets were impacted in a multitude of ways. At Creature Concierge, we transformed many of our service processes and integrated personal protection equipment (PPEs) supplies to optimize everyone's safety. We sent email blasts to pet owners to inform them about our new, COVID-19 compliance safety protocols so parents would feel safe as we entered their homes to care for their pets. We provided critical Center for Disease Control (CDC) updates to inform pet owners of news regarding the virus and their pet's health.

In addition, we offered two new services: deliveries and emergency boarding. If parents were quarantined, we delivered pet supplies and medications to them. If parents were hospitalized, we offered to take care of their pets until they made it home. Elective surgeries, for pets and people, were delayed so pets had to be more closely supervised.

While home visits went down during the COVID-19 quarantine period, the phone calls from parents increased. *What's wrong? Fido doesn't have a good appetite. Where can I take Spot for treatment since my vet clinic is closed? Is it safe to delay my dog's vaccines? I think our dog swallowed chocolate; what do we do?*

Why is it that so many dog owners don't have what they need to ensure the survival of their pets after common mishaps or in dire situations? It's not because they don't care; quite the contrary: it's because they aren't prepared. Think about it. If you want a dog, with few exceptions, you can fill out a simple form and adopt one out of a local shelter or from an area rescue group. You don't go through a class to learn about pet care, there are no practice sessions that review dog safety, there is no how-to manual handed over with your adoption credentials. It's trial by error. It shouldn't be. It no longer has to be.

This segment of the book is designed to help you prepare for the care and well-being of your dog before the next disaster or any medical emergency occurs.

This portion of your guide will focus on how to:

- Prepare Medical Paperwork
- Prepare a First Aid Kit
- Prepare Your First Aid Skills
- Prepare for Natural Disasters
- Prepare for Medical Expenses

CHAPTER 2

Prepare Your Pet's Medical Care Paperwork

Your friend is caring for your puppy and yellow-headed parrot. Your friend opens the parrot cage to clean it out and add fresh food and water. The parrot escapes, but his wings are clipped so he can't fly far. The bird falls to the floor where he attacks the curious puppy. Your friend rescues the dog and rushes him to the vet. Unfortunately, the veterinarian listed by the parents only treats birds so your friend had to find a veterinarian emergency clinic for your dog.

It is common for pet parents to provide emergency information so caretakers know where to go in case of an emergency. However, too often this information is missing critical details or is outdated. I've made it easy to prepare for pet-related disasters, accidents, illnesses, and injuries by providing you with the critical documents and resources to fill out on all your pets in advance.

Prepare Medical Emergency Documents

The American Pet Products Association 2019 survey revealed 67 percent of the US households, about 85 million families, own a pet. If I could, all 85 million pet owners would organize key medical information for each pet they own. What information is needed may not always be obvious, so I've provided an Emergency Pet Resource Document (EPRD) to make it clear what essential data to prepare. An EPRD is a single form with crucial medical emergency information. You might also carry the same information on your smartphone.

Most pet owners will list their veterinarian's name, address, phone number, and website. What parents often fail to consider is that they may not be the one using this information. It may be an extended family member, a neighbor who uses a different veterinarian or a pet sitter. Adding other details, like what services your vet offers and how far away their office is from your home, is very important.

At Creature Concierge, our pet parents are required to fill out details about every pet in the family. Your Emergency Pet Resource Document should make it clear if the primary vet you've listed services all the pets you own. Many veterinarians only care for dogs and cats. Exotic pets like birds, hamsters, mice, rabbits, snakes, spiders, turtles, hedgehogs, and potbellied pigs, to name a few, may have a completely different veterinarian in a separate location. This form can help anyone caring for your pet at any place (including a daycare/boarding facility) to take action properly and quickly for your pet.

Details about area pet emergency facilities are equally important for timely, prudent decision-making. If your dog needs care but your vet is closed, do you know where to go? Is there one pet hospital that is better than another in your area? Does the pet hospital have vet specialists (orthopedists, neurologists, etc.) on staff and the kind of equipment needed for both minor and major emergencies? Which facilities are capable of conducting all lab tests and diagnostic tests in-house, including taking X-rays, MRIs, CAT scans, or sonograms?

One more thing: when seconds count, a form is only helpful if the information is current. While our great nation was dealing with the war against COVID-19, many of our area veterinarian clinics either closed or changed their service hours and protocols. In anticipation of this happening, my team and I updated our area pet hospital data to reflect what facilities were still open (and at what hours) throughout the crisis. Update your emergency documents to reflect changes: a new dog, a new doctor, where to purchase unique things like compound prescriptions or what pharmacy has your dog's critical medications like insulin. A sample EPRD follows to illustrate what information is needed on the form.

Prepare Your Pet's Medical Care Paperwork

(SAMPLE) EMERGENCY PET RESOURCE DOCUMENT FOR:

<u>Pet: Fido Johnson</u>

Pet Sitter 911 #:	(000) 000-0000
Veterinarian:	Dr. Jane Doe
	So & So Southside Vet Clinic
Phone #:	(000) 000-0000
Address:	000 Riverside Drive, Dallas, Texas 00000
# Miles Away:	4 miles from Fido's home
Hours:	Monday-Friday 8 am to 6 pm
	Saturday 9 AM to 4 PM Closed Sunday.
Services:	General veterinary medicine. Minor surgery.
Pet Types:	Dogs, cats, birds
Website:	www.southsidevet.com
Hospital #1:	**XYZ VETERINARY HOSPITAL**
Phone #:	(000) 000-0000 8 am to 6 pm
	(000) 000-0000 After 5 pm
Address:	000 Trinity Drive, Addison, Texas 00000
# Miles Away:	12. 5 miles from Fido's home
Hours:	24 hours Monday–Sunday
Services:	Orthopedics, Oncology
Hours:	24 hours Monday–Sunday
Pet Types:	Dogs, cats, exotics, birds
Website:	www. XYZVet.com
Hospital #2:	**ABC VETERINARY PET HOSPITAL**
Phone #:	(000) 000-0000
Address:	000 Midway Blvd, West Plano, Texas
# Miles Away:	10 miles from Fido's home
Services:	General veterinary emergency medicine
Hours:	Monday–Friday 5 pm to 8 am
	Saturday and Sunday, 24 hours
Pet Types:	Dogs, cats, birds, most wildlife, licensed for water birds
Website:	www.ABCVetPet.com

Medications

Time	Treatment	Dose	Details	Source
6 am	Insulin	8 units	Inject on left side	CVS, Parkwood
6 pm	Insulin	8 units	Inject on right side	(000) 000-0000
6 am	Apoquel	1, 16 mg tablet	Inside ½ pill pocket	Dr. XYZ

ALLERGIES: _____
(Meds & Food) _____

PET INSURANCE: Name _____
Policy #_____

The following is a blank form you can use for each of your pets.

Prepare Your Pet's Medical Care Paperwork

EMERGENCY PET RESOURCE DOCUMENT:

Pet Name: _____

Pet Sitter 24 Hour #: _____
Veterinarian(s): _____

Phone #: _____
Website: _____
Address: _____

Miles Away: _____
Hours: _____
Services: _____
Pet Types: _____

Pet Hospital #1: _____
Phone #: _____

Website: _____
Address: _____

Miles Away: _____
Hours: _____

Services: _____

Pet Types: _____

Pet Hospital #2: _____
Phone #: _____

Website: _____
Address: _____

Miles Away: _____

5-STEP CANINE CARE

Hours: _____

Services: _____

Pet Types: _____
_____

Medications

Time	Treatment	Dose	Details	Source

ALLERGIES: _____
(Meds & Food) _____

PET INSURANCE: Name _____ Policy #: _____ Phone #: _____

Prepare a Medical Treatment & Transport Release Form

There is one more form to prepare: a Medical Treatment & Transport Release Form (MTTR). This form provides several critical pieces of data:

- Permission to transport your pet to a veterinarian or vet hospital facility during an emergency
- The name of the medical facility the parents prefer to use for veterinary care
- Authorization to pay for emergency/health related emergencies up to a certain amount

Whether you're traveling for business or pleasure, you want to make sure your dog's caretaker has a signed copy of this form. Your caretaker may be a family member, a neighbor, a professional pet care specialist, a boarding facility representative, and/or a family veterinarian. A sample MTTR Form follows. You can develop your own or use the one provided in this guide.

MEDICAL TREATMENT & TRANSPORT RELEASE FORM

Date: _____
Pet(s): _____
Pet Parent(s): _____

In case of an emergency, I hereby authorize my designated pet care agent _____ _____ to do the following for my pet:

- pay for veterinarian care and emergency veterinarian treatment for my pet in my absence, up to $_____;
- pay for scheduled groomer, non-emergency vet visits, pet food supplies, daycare, boarding services in my absence up to $_____;
- pick up and drop off my pet to designated owner-approved suppliers (groomer, daycare/boarding site).

My signature below is confirmation that I understand my designated agent will be notified immediately of any transport and/or medical/health-related pet needs. I understand that my agent will be allowed to transport my pet to my designated veterinarian or emergency pet center. Furthermore, I agree to reimburse the agent for all aforementioned payments.

Parent Name: _____

Parent Signature: _____

Date: _____

Prepare Your Pet's Medical Care Paperwork

PAYMENT OPTIONS

Credit Card # (ending in): _____ (last 4 digits only)

This card is to be used to purchase pet supplies and medical services between: _____ & _____ (List start and end dates.)

Parent's signature of approval to use credit card: _____

Date: _____

ACTION

- Get the sample EPRD, provided for you in this guide, filled out and distributed to the humans in your life that help care for your pets.
- Set an alarm on your phone for one week from today as a reminder to make sure your forms are completed and distributed to all necessary parties. If you own an Alexa, Siri, or Google Assistant, program them to remind you of key pet care deadlines. If not, an old fashioned, sticky note reminder written on your household calendar will work too.
- Use a mailing pouch or multi-paper plastic sleeve to store all pertinent documents:
    - A copy of the most recent pet immunizations
    - A copy of your EPRD form for each pet
    - A copy of your MTTR form for all pets

CHAPTER 3

Prepare a First Aid Kit

It was dusk, and my little dog, Shasta, and I were heading in the house. We lived, at the time, in a condo in Reno, Nevada that backed up to Rattlesnake Mountain. I was just walking into the house when I heard a loud yelp and turned to see Shasta racing toward me. It didn't take a clear view of her to know what had happened. Shasta had been skunked. I guess a skunk had found its way under the backyard fence. She got sprayed right in the face.

I scooped her up (she only weighed about nine pounds and change) and headed for the kitchen sink. My neighbor Jennifer was visiting at the time and raced to the store to purchase large cans of tomato juice. At the time, we thought that was the best way to de-skunk my little Shasta. While Jennifer was gone, I called a local emergency pet hospital where I was told to first flush her eyes with water thoroughly and repeatedly. Next, they told me to bathe her in a hydrogen peroxide solution. The recipe follows.

- 1 quart of 3% hydrogen peroxide solution
- ¼ cup of baking soda
- 1 to 2 teaspoons of dishwashing liquid

Quickly mix well and work into your dog's coat before the skunk oil (spray) settles into the dog's fur. Leave on for five minutes. Rinse with warm water.

Tip: If you do not have any hydrogen peroxide, you can use two parts water with one-part cider vinegar. Soak your dog's coat and rub in this mixture for four to five minutes and then rinse thoroughly. Or, keep a bottle of Nature's Miracle® Skunk Odor Remover on hand.

Prepare a First Aid Kit for Your Dog

It is best not to use your human kit supplies for pet-related medical emergencies. Some products and medications cannot be used on your dog. Either buy a first aid kit designed and packed specifically for your pet, or develop one on your own. Work with your vet or a Pet Tech Trainer (more on that in Chapter 9) for help.

One method of making sure you have what is needed for a superior dog first aid kit is to create one yourself, packed with the tools and treatments you are likely to need. Don't forget a first aid manual that includes instructional tips (see some of my favorites in this section of the book) to help get you or any pet sitter through most emergencies. Be sure to consider your geographic area and hobbies. By building a kit around your hobbies (mountain hiking in Colorado, for example) and your terrain (West Texas: rattlesnake country), you are more likely to have what you need.

Have you thought about what you would need in your dog's first aid kit? Consider that some of the supplies needed are suitable for typical home-related emergencies whereas others are recommended for pet owners who are more active outdoors with their pets. Although many of these supplies are commonly found in most homes, you want to have them organized in one kit for quick access. If you and your dog enjoy hiking, camping, boating, running, or traveling together, your first aid kit will need items associated with those activities.

Tools to Pack in Your Dog's First Aid Kit

Bandages:	Six, 24-gauge rolls of latex free, non-stick bandages.
Blanket:	Mylar thermal foil blankets from Swiss Safe work great to help retain body heat, shielding users against hypothermia and shock.
Bowl:	Collapsible bowl for water to fight off dehydration.
Card:	An old grocery store, plastic discount card to flick out bee stingers.

Cold Pack:	An instant cold pack can be used to reduce swelling around a wound or broken limb.
Cotton:	Cotton balls and extra long cotton applicators for applying medicine or cleaning wounds.
Clippers:	Ideally a battery-operated clipper with trimmer to remove hair around wounds, remove fur matted from blood, or clear fur around an area to make it easier to keep wounds clean.
E-Collar:	Also known as "Elizabethan Collars" are used when you need to prevent your dog from accessing a wound area. Pack an inflatable e-collar sized for your dog. Deflated, they take up very little room. However, the inflatable e-collars are not always big enough (in diameter) to work for all situations so ideally you will also have a traditional rubber cone-shaped e-collar too.
Flashlight:	A dependable, extra bright flashlight. Too many smartphone users believe their phone 'light' will be enough. It isn't. Pack a compact, bright flashlight (at least 750- to 1000-plus lumens) that will illuminate wounds clearly and light up rescue areas effectively.
Gauze:	• 1 dozen, 4" x 4" gauze pads • 2 rolls of 2" x 2" gauze • 1 roll of 4"x 4" gauze
Gloves:	At least two pairs of non-Latex, disposable gloves to avoid contaminating an injury you are trying to treat.
Leash:	One leather leash (more durable) with snap clip in good condition. Add one nylon slip leash. The slip leash is designed to quickly and easily secure a dog that does not have a collar on or has lost/broken his collar.
Magnifier:	A magnifying glass to make it easier to see thorns or tiny details around a wound.

5-STEP CANINE CARE

Muzzle:	Injured animals will sometimes bite when treated. Having a muzzle available keeps you safe while helping your pet.
Pill Box:	This is a water- or moisture-proof organizer with multiple compartments, including a space for syringes.
Rope:	Roll of durable, nylon parachute rope that can be used as an emergency leash or to hoist your dog up a steep incline
Scissors:	Both standard scissors and bandage forceps for both left- and right-handed people.
Splint:	Include a Rapid Application SAM Medical® Splint to securely and safely brace broken or injured limbs.
Syringes:	Include at least three in sterile sleeves. These can be used to flush punctures and open wounds as well as flush debris out of eyes and to deliver liquid medications.
Thermometer:	To determine if your pet has a fever (generally indicating they are fighting some type of infection). A mercury-free, rectal thermometer is preferable.
Tourniquet:	You can use an extra wide slip leash if you don't have anything else.
Towel:	A microfiber towel is best. It has greater absorption and it dries out faster. Use to dry pets that fall in frigid water or when they get wet in very cold temperatures.
Trauma Pad:	One box of sterile, absorbent trauma dressing pads to help stop bleeding.
Tweezers:	To pull out splinters, thorns, ticks, etc.
Water:	To ensure your pets remain hydrated; to cleanse wounds.

Wrap:	Add at least two large rolls of self-adhering, water-repellent first aid wrap. These won't stick to your dog's fur.

Treatments to Pack in Your Kit:

In a perfect world, you can reach your veterinarian or local pet hospital professionals if your dog is ill or injured. However, if immediate care is necessary and veterinary care is not available, this guide is designed to help you know what to do and what treatment to apply for common emergency situations. Many of these products can be purchased at a local store or online at Chewy.com or at 1-800-Pet-Meds.

Antibiotic:	Medi-first triple antibiotic ointment to kill bacteria on wounds to prevent infection.
Anti-Diarrheal:	Pet Pectillin® is an anti-diarrhea supplement for dogs and cats. Short-term use of Kaopectate® or Pepcid® is also an option. More severe diarrhea may require the use of Endosorb® (a prescription drug) you would get from your veterinarian.
Antiseptic:	Include antiseptic wipes or spray like Vetericyn Plus® Antimicrobial pet wound/skin care.
Benadryl:	Contains the antihistamine Diphenhydramine that can help reduce swelling due to allergies or an allergic reaction to a sting. Do not use anything but regular Benadryl® as other products for colds and flu may contain other ingredients like Xylitol, which can be fatal if ingested by a dog.
Clotting:	Bottle of ClotIt® blood clotting powder to stop or slow excessive bleeding. Clotit can be used for dogs but not cats. Remedy+Recovery™, This is a styptic powder that can be sprinkled on superficial cuts and scrapes to stop bleeding. Miracle Care Kwik-Stop® Liquid Gel can also be used for this purpose.

Disinfectant:	Chlorhexidine (Diacetate) Solution diluted to .05% for cleaning wound areas. Dilution: is 2 tablespoons of Chlorhexidine Solution per gallon of water. Apply, wipe dry with sterile gauze.
Dressing:	EMT First Aid Spray can be applied to serve as an invisible bandage.
Ear Rinse:	Virbac Epi-Otic Advanced® ear cleanser. Curaseb™ Chlorhexidine antifungal, antibacterial, and anti-yeast wipes are also handy to have in your ear treatment kits.
Eye Rinse:	One large bottle of Bausch & Lomb Eye Rinse® or Simple Saline Ophthalmic® saline solution and OcuSoft® eye wash can be used to flush wounds as well as clean eyes of debris or to flush eyes out if your pet is sprayed in the face by a skunk.
Peroxide:	Hydrogen peroxide (1 quart of 3% hydrogen peroxide), ¼ cup of baking soda and 1 teaspoon dishwashing soap can be combined to treat skunk smell on your pet. Tip: Do *not* store this solution as it can explode if left in a bottle.
Indigestion:	Milk of Magnesia can be used with dogs to treat mild indigestion, gastric reflux, and constipation.
Lubricant:	One tube. Your pet's temperature will be more accurate if taken rectally. A lubricant like Surgilube® gel or Dynarex Dynalube® pads will make this task more comfortable for your pet.
Poison:	Universal Animal Antidote® (UAA) gel as an emergency solution to combat ingesting poisons (insecticides for example). ToxiBan® contains Sorbitol, activated charcoal, and kaolin that work together to treat pets that have swallowed poison.
Probiotics:	NaturVet® Digestive Enzymes Plus Probiotic and Pro-Pectalin paste can often reduce mild diarrhea by inhibiting the growth of harmful bacteria.

Vetericyn: Vetericyn® Plus Hydro Gel for wound and Skin Care. It's non-toxic apply to cuts, sores, dry skin/allergies.

First Aid Kits to Purchase

If you feel a bit overwhelmed by this list of recommended First Aid supplies, consider purchasing a kit that is already assembled for you. You can always add to it. Be sure to select a first aid kit suited for the activities you do most with your dog (hiking, water sports, for example). Some kits to consider:

- Adventure Medical Kits Me & My Dog (by MidwayUSA©)
- Curicyn™ Pet Care First Aid Kit
- Kurgo® RSG Dog First Aid Kit
- RC Pet Products© Pet First Aid Kit
- Sporting Dog First Aid Kit (L.L. Bean©)
- Thrive© First Aid Kit

Most of these kits come with a first aid manual. If not, there is a miniature guide produced by Jones & Bartlett Learning that you might consider buying. It's easy to carry in a pocket and pretty comprehensive. It can be ordered on Amazon or at http://www.jblearning.com/. One more thing: it is important to update your emergency kit to reflect changes in your environment. For example, during the COVID-19 pandemic, virtually all quality Personal Protection Equipment (PPEs) went directly from the manufacturers to hospitals and other medical-related facilities. This was not only prudent but also critical if we were to protect our first line responders, doctors, and nurses. However, as my team, along with other pet care specialists and workers prepared to go back to work, it was abundantly clear that we also needed PPEs in order to work safely.

We had a unique advantage at Creature Concierge in that we already had an online product store where we sold personalized pet products. We also had suppliers worldwide to source virtually anything, so we started selling PPEs in our online store to our Creature Concierge clients and, over time, to other vet clinics and small business owners in the region.

We purchased these supplies as soon as the COVID-19 virus news infiltrated the daily news. Are you watching for impending emergencies that may require a change in your supplies? Are you still looking for affordable PPEs? We have them available to anyone at our sister company, CEO Wired: http://www.ceowired.com.

Having the proper equipment and supplies you need is so important. However, it's no substitute for applying first aid fundamentals in the moment. To that end, I encourage all dog owners, pet caretakers, dog walkers, and daycare/boarding facility employees to take a pet first aid/CPR class. It's great to have a guide that walks you through the steps to take in a particular type of emergency. A good first aid/CPR class enables you to apply what you learn and practice first aid methods so they come naturally in an emergency situation. In the next chapter, I will go into details on the course I recommend.

CHAPTER 4

Prepare Your Emergency Skills

On the eve of July 4, 2009, my precious little dog, Shasta, died in my arms. While I attempted CPR to save her, I had no previous formal training. I did what I could, but my efforts were futile. Losing Shasta was catastrophic to me. She was my "child," my most treasured friend, and dearest companion. Her death was not only a terrible loss for me but also a very sad wakeup call that made me realize how poorly prepared I was for most pet emergencies. Since then, I not only took a CPR/first aid class (for dogs and cats), but I also became a national Pet Tech first aid trainer to teach other pet lovers how to care for creature kids during an emergency.

Why is it so important for pet owners to have fundamental first aid training for pets? Dog owners deal with common accidents every day. WebMD (for pets) points out that there are almost 214,000 cases of pet poisoning a year; the Animal Channel reports more than 1.2 million dogs are killed on the roads each year. How many of these accidents could have been prevented (with better dog owner training) or the outcomes improved after these accidents if parents had sound medical preparation and first aid training?

Now, imagine the need for these skills in a natural disaster. An F4 tornado storms through your entire neighborhood and surrounding area. There would be no electrical power and roads would be blocked. You and your family would be trapped in your home (or what's left of it), access to water and food supplies would virtually vanish, and many people and pets would have injuries. It could be many days before help of any kind can reach you. This may seem like an extreme situation, but all sorts of emergencies happen to people and pets every day: boating, hiking, traveling, playing at the dog park, while fetching, swimming, to name a few. When disaster strikes and minutes count, first aid training may be what it takes to stabilize your pet until you can get them to a veterinary clinic or hospital where the professionals can take over.

Sign up and attend a local first aid training class for pets. Learn how to administer CPR for your dog. Local American Red Cross chapters in most communities offer pet first aid courses; however, there are other organizations that provide this service, too. My favorite pet first aid/CPR course is provided nationwide by certified trainers. The pet care course I recommend was developed by Pet Tech (www.pettech.net) and designed to help pet owners, animal rescuers, animal shelter employees, and vet assistants learn first aid fundamentals for cats and dogs. Pet Tech has an online "location search" feature so you can find an instructor somewhere in your area.

Regardless of what class you take, a quality course should include instruction on:

- How to deal effectively with burns, bites, bleeding
- Administering CPR
- What first aid measures to take if a dog ingests poison, starts to experience seizures, or is bitten by a snake
- Reviewing what equipment to use for a tourniquet
- How to muzzle and restrain a dog safely
- Preventative wellness measures to take for senior dogs
- Dental care for dogs
- What to do if your dog is choking
- So much more

Here are some emergency care tips we've learned and applied through our years of pet care. These tips are reflective of some of the things you will learn in a first aid class:

- How to remain calm during an emergency situation. Your dog will already be anxious if sick or injured, so what demeanor you project will either minimize his or her anxiety or exacerbate it, making it tougher to treat them.
- Do not crush a tick when taking it out. Store it in a sanitized container in case your vet needs to test it for Lyme Disease, Rocky Mountain Spotted Fever, Tularemia, or Ehrlichiosis.

- Should your pet get stung by a bee or wasp, first remove the stinger. Do not use tweezers to remove bee stingers. Tweezers compress the stinger and push more venom into your pet.
  - Use a butter knife or credit card to flick out the stinger at the skin surface level.
  - Flush the area. If you see the area start swelling, see your pet vomit or drool excessively, and/or become feverish, they may be going into anaphylactic shock. If so, try to get to your vet or vet hospital.
    - To buy time, you can open a Benadryl gel capsule and give the contents to your pet.
    - NOTE: calculate the dose of Benadryl using this online dose calculator: https://www.preventivevet.com/dogs/bee-and-wasp-stings-be-prepared#benadryldosagecalculator
- Bandages: be careful what you apply directly to your pet's fur. Some bandages and medical tape are not designed for direct application to fur and would be very painful to remove.
- Just a reminder: a normal temperature for dogs is 99.5 to 102.5 degrees Fahrenheit.
- If your pet ingested some type of poison, first alert your vet then call pet poison control at: (888) 426-4435.
- Do not use hydrogen peroxide to clean a wound. It often slows healing.
- Splints can be made out of a stick, dowel, ruler, or broom handle.
- An in-home quick remedy for treating stings on your pet is a thick layer of baking soda and water or an oatmeal bath and then a baking soda/water pack.
- Eliminating skunk spray: Hydrogen Peroxide Solution (1 quart of 3%), ¼ cup of baking soda and 1 teaspoon liquid dishwashing soap. Glove up, mix well, and work into your pet's coat. Rinse and repeat.
- Your dog and cat's gut contains 70 percent of all immune cells, so keep their gut healthy with a well-balanced diet. (See chapter 23 for more details.) A daily probiotic is another way to contribute to the overall health of your dog.

- Do not use cold packs directly against your dog's skin to bring their temperature down, as it could shock their system.

Go online today and find a quality pet first aid/CPR class. If you live in or around the DFW region of Texas, feel free to go to JetPetTech.com and sign up for our next course. I wish I had done so. CPR may have kept Shasta alive long enough for me to get her to an emergency room where a veterinarian team could have saved her. So, don't wait. Get ready today for whatever happens to your pet tomorrow.

CHAPTER 5

Prepare for Disasters

I was born and raised in Texas. Storms are something you learn to expect. If you live along the Texas coast, you prepare for hurricanes. If you're in the panhandle of Texas, you prepare for snow storms. If you live in central Texas, you plan for tornadoes and hail. It's a big state with a virtual *buffet* of natural disasters.

Whereas emergency preparation is generally focused on an immediate response to save your pet after an incident (your dog is attacked by a bobcat or your dog punctures his leg when he falls on a sharp object), disaster planning is about long-term survival. Whether a virus, a hurricane, an earthquake, an avalanche, or some other disaster, everyone should prepare a plan to deal with it. This chapter will help make sure all your pet's needs are addressed before disaster strikes.

Records & Notifications:

Make a copy of your pet's annual immunization records. Include a photo of your dog and a photo of your family with your dog. It makes it easier for animal rescue groups to identify your pet. The family photos (along with adoption papers) will help to prove ownership of your dog. Seal these items inside a zip-closed plastic baggie or take them to your local office supply store and have them laminated. Use duct tape on all four sides to adhere these records and photos to your pet's crate. Use a permanent marker to write your pet's name and your last name on the crate.

Tags:

In addition to your dog or cat's rabies tags (required by law) make sure your pet has a tag with their name and your contact phone number on it. Make sure all tag information is legible and updated.

Collars:

In addition to your pet's standard collar, consider placing a location collar on your pet prior to a pending disaster. These collars have everything from lights on them to locator beacons. Should you get separated from your dog, you want to make sure other people can easily see them and help you find them. I've listed (below) some of the specialty collars on the market. Select the option best suited for disasters in your region. For example, if you live in a flooding zone, you want a waterproof collar. If you and your dog like to hike in snowy, mountainous areas, your dog needs a collar that can transmit a signal in extreme cold temperatures or under mounds of snow.

Some of the disaster preparation collars to consider:
SportDOG® Locator Beacon
Pieps TX600 Dog Transmitter©
Findster®
Illumiseen.com©

Chips:

Does your pet have a microchip? If not, get one. Microchips are essentially a miniscule radio-frequency identification (RFID) device embedded under your dog's skin. It requires no power source. If your dog is found, vets and rescuers use a wand to scan your pet. If chipped, a tiny signal transmits your dog's microchip ID number tied to your contact information.

- When was the last time you went to your vet to make sure the chip still works?
- What name comes up when the ID number is looked up in the system? Is it your contact information or the contact data from the shelter you adopted your dog from?
- Is your contact phone number correct? Did you change it after you got a new phone number? If you use an external chip device like Findster®, be sure to alert the pet locator service company of any new home address or phone numbers.

Notices:

Make sure you have notices in your home windows to alert rescuers and first responders that there are pets inside. These are mini signs that cling to glass. They usually display a graphic of a dog or cat with a message to find them in case of a disaster. You can purchase these online in a variety of sizes. Our favorites can be found at the links below. The best signs have a graphic of a cat, a dog, a bird and a rabbit on it with a box next to each, so first responders and rescuers know what kind of pet you have and how many of each are in the home. If you're traveling in a mobile/RV home, make sure you have one of these posted on a vehicle window.

Here are a few other notices to consider:

- KeepDoggieSafe.com
- Being Stray.com
- iHeartDogs.com
- Pet Alert Safety Fire Rescue Sticker

Supplies:

In addition to the first aid kit items listed in Chapter 4, you should also have the supplies needed to care for your pet's daily needs. Use the list below to prepare. Note: don't forget the supplies you may need for typical disasters in your region. For example, if your area is prone to flooding, make sure you have life jackets for your pets. If you have a large dog that is either injured or must be carried like your other pets because the area is too dangerous for walking due to flooding or dangerous debris, have what you need on hand to carry them. Carrying a sixty-eight-pound dog in a crate is tough. Purchase something like a Pack-a-Paw (www.mountaindogware.com). This is a lightweight harness specifically designed to enable people to carry their canine (hands-free) during an emergency evacuation situation. You may want a separate case for carrying the pertinent supplies (below).

A few to consider:

- Bring Your Dog 5 Piece Pet Travel Bag
- Overland Dog Gear Week Away Tote Pet Travel Bag
- Teamoy Double Layer Dog Travel Bag

- Solvit HomeAway Pet Travel Organizer

Pack for Dogs

Food: At least a seven-day supply. If canned food, include a manual can opener and a permanent ink marker. Use the marker to write the date of the food on the can.

Water: At least a ten-day supply. Tip: About a half-gallon per day for small dogs; one gallon a day for large dogs.

Waste bags: To pick up and discard waste that will attract flies and rodents.

Comforts: Favorite toy, bed, blanket.

Crate: A transport crate. Don't forget to adhere critical records (defined earlier in this chapter) somewhere on the crate. A Portable Pet Tent (like the one made by Marketfleet.com) may also be helpful.

Restraint: A harness (not just a collar), a leather leash (nylon leashes melt too easily) and a slip leash. Should Fido get loose, it may be easier to snag them on a slip leash. Replace with harness and leather leash once you catch your dog.

Medications

Make a list of all your dog's medications and include this information with your other documents in the zip-closed plastic bag before you tape it to your dog's crate. Purchase a waterproof (or at least a moisture-proof) medicine container. Cikava sells one that also includes a compartment for syringes. You should have at least a two-week supply of all meds in this container. If your pet is on insulin, make sure you have a way to keep the insulin cool. The Frio Insulin Cooling Case is a perfect solution, as it doesn't require refrigeration. It is an insulated pouch where you can store any type of medicine that must stay cool during a disaster. Don't forget your dog's flea, tick, and heartworm meds. Place tape on the inside lid of your pill container and write the date you packed it on the tape.

Exit Plan and Housing

Sit down with your family and review a clear plan for getting out of your neighborhood should streets be blocked. Where did you store all your supplies? Does everyone in the family know where you have emergency disaster items stored? How are you transporting the items? Remember you may be carting everything around under difficult circumstances. Look for a durable, lightweight, waterproof trunk on wheels. Where do you meet your family (and pet) after a disaster? Communicate these details with extended family members and, just as importantly, with your immediate neighbors who may have to help you reunite with your pets if you're not at home when disaster strikes. Once you have an exit plan, where do you go? Many emergency shelters and hotels don't allow pets. These are the topics to discuss with family and friends in advance.

Reminders

Set an alert on your phone to go off every six months. Many people do this as a reminder to change the batteries in their home smoke alarm. When this alert goes off, (and after you check your smoke alarm), check expiration dates and/or replace the following items in your disaster supply kit:

- Pet food
- Pet medications
- Batteries in flashlights and in your emergency radio

CHAPTER 6

Prepare for Medical Expenses

I was taking care of two dogs about seven miles from my home when I got a frantic call from my 91-year-old mother. She said a dachshund bit Sunny, her five-pound, Apple Head Chihuahua. I raced to the house, scooped him up and rushed him to the veterinary hospital. One of the emergency nurses was waiting for me at the curb. Apple Head Chihuahuas have a soft spot on the top of their head (called a molera) that doesn't always seal up. The miniature dachshund that bit Sunny weighed only ten pounds, but penetrated the soft spot. We waited at the hospital for the surgical team to stabilize Sunny. He needed surgery to reduce the swelling on his brain. Sunny was in the care of the best surgeons in the region, but he died during surgery.

I had two things that gave me some comfort after his passing. One, we had pet insurance for him, so even though the medical costs were exorbitant (over $9,000), neither my mother nor I had to let Sunny die because we couldn't afford emergency treatment. Sadly, this happens all the time. People want to save their dogs, but they just don't have enough money for expensive emergency treatment. Two, imagine how heartbreaking it was to lose this tiny, two-year-old dog. Now imagine how much worse it would have been to spend nearly $10,000 to save him only to be in debt for that much money after he's gone. We don't want anyone to be in this situation. This chapter is designed to educate pet owners on what options are available to mitigate the negative impact of veterinary expenses (standard or emergency).

We love to teach parents about preventative care that will reduce annual, medical-related expenses. If you have not yet selected a pet, consider choosing a creature kid that is statistically likely to be less expensive. The ASPCA reported that the average annual cost of care for a large dog is $875, for a cat is $670, for a small bird is $200, and so on. **Tip:** A mixed-breed dog, between ten and twenty pounds, is typically the least expensive dog to own.

Pet insurance, available since Veterinary Pet Insurance Services, Inc. (VPI) began offering policies in 1980, is one method for mitigating pet care costs. We also encourage pet owners to budget funds each year for their pet's annual checkup, vaccinations, flea, tick and heartworm prevention, as well as for quality food and supplements.

All the planning in the world is not enough, sometimes, because creature kids, much like human kids, can get sick and/or injured. This may require complicated surgery or long-term treatment, resulting in serious expenses. The average cost of emergency veterinary surgery for dogs is between $800 and $1,500. The number one pet health issues reported by parents are skin problems that can cost up to $5,000. Parents with pet insurance will sail through these difficult times without ever suffering post-procedure debt. Conversely, those that don't may have to address debt and/or euthanize their pet prematurely.

Why Get Pet Insurance

- To prevent premature euthanizing of your pet because you can't afford treatment for chronic illnesses (for example, cancer)
- To enable you to pay for the best emergency services on a timely basis without worry
- To reduce standard care costs for annual wellness checkups and lab tests

There are more than a dozen pet insurance companies in the marketplace, and they write more than a billion dollars in policies a year. You want to choose carefully as some have too many variables (exceptions) to be worth the monthly premium. Having said that, there are several pet insurance plans worth buying. Key to selecting the best plan for your pet is first asking the right questions.

Questions To Ask Your (Potential) Pet Insurance Policy Representative:

- What is covered under the policy?

- Preventative care?
- Annual wellness exams?
- Treatments for chronic illnesses? (Ex: cancer)
- Surgeries? (Emergency, Ligament?)
- Post-surgical therapy?
- Congenital conditions? Pre-existing conditions? Hereditary conditions?
- Dental care/cleaning?
- Prescriptions?
- End-of-life services: euthanasia? Burial?
- When does coverage start? Is there a waiting period on any services?
- Are there age limits?
- What do you need from me to ensure my pet qualifies for your policy? (A vet exam? A form from my vet? A DNA test?)
- Is there an annual deductible? Is there a per-incident deductible?
- Are there co-pays?
- Is there a per-incident cap? An annual cap? A lifetime cap?
- Will the policy cover treatment for breed specific conditions? For example, hip dysplasia for your German Shepherd (a breed known for hip dysplasia issues).
- If you have a rescue dog with no specific breed data, will this impact covering breed-specific conditions?
- Are there any pre-existing conditions you do not cover, or a waiting period before you will cover them?
- What are your monthly premium costs? Are payments automatically withdrawn from my account or do I receive a bill each month? Can I choose the day of the month when the payment is due?
- How do I file a claim? What is the process? Where do I get a claim form?
- Do you pay my veterinarian bill directly or reimburse me after I pay the vet bill? If you reimburse me, what percentage of the bill will you pay? How is the reimbursement calculated? How long does it take to get reimbursed?
- Can I change my policy after it starts?

- Can I view my pet's records, reimbursements, and medical documents? Can I update them online?
- Is there an 800 number I can call for questions? For help? Is a person available to help me during an after-hours emergency/weekends?
- What if I want to add a pet to my policy? What if I want to cancel my policy?
- Do you offer accident only insurance? If so, how could this benefit my older and/or sick dog?
- Is there any benefit program for referring new clients to you?

More pet parents are realizing it may be prudent to get insurance for their beloved companions. In 2018, 2.43 million pets were insured in the U.S. and Canada. This was a 17.1 percent increase over 2017. Review and compare the pet insurance programs. Some are well worth what you pay in monthly premiums. Do your own research so you understand which policy is best for your budget and your specific pet/breed. Use our list of questions to make sure you get the most critical, comparative information to evaluate the merits of each policy objectively. If you look at comparison charts on the Internet, be sure to note the source behind these charts. Some pet insurance advisory sources have business alliances with the companies *evaluating* them. Having evaluated the merits of all the industries' top options (including those listed below), we feel like (in most cases) Healthy Paws and Petplan are two of the best. They offer competitively priced plans, payout on a timely basis, provide coverage for dogs of all ages and so much more. I've provided a list of other pet insurance companies to consider before making a decision.

Embrace
FIGO
Healthy Paws
PetFirst
PetPlan
PetsBest
Trupanion

Other Funding Sources for Reducing Pet Healthcare Costs

Some of the obvious (but often forgotten) methods of reducing pet medical costs: attention and prevention. Pay attention to changes in your dog so you catch health problems early. Getting treatment before a disease or injury progresses will make it cost less money to treat. Review the Attention to Signs segment of this guide so you know if your pet is displaying the first signs of a serious illness. Apply what we teach in the "prevention" section of this guide to avoid the accidents that often result in expensive emergency care. When your pet is diagnosed with a serious injury or illness with treatments beyond your means, here are other options for paying for medical care.

Waggle.org

Waggle is a *crowdfunding* site, a virtual community of pet lovers on one online platform. They work together to raise funds for parents with pets in a medical crisis to help them avoid economic euthanasia. Over 500,000 pets in the U.S. are impacted in some way by the need for veterinary care but the treatment is cost prohibitive for the pet owner. In far too many of these situations, the owners have to euthanize their pet rather than save them. Waggle can help prevent this, if you find yourself in this situation. Or, if you wish to help others, you can join Waggle as a patron.

CareCredit.com

CareCredit is a credit card designed to help pet owners finance medical expenses. Accepted by more than 225,000 healthcare providers, this card provides an affordable (0 interest introductory period) payment option for larger veterinary related expenses. **Tip:** Other cards with similar benefits are the H5 WellnessPlus Card and The Citi Health Card. The latter enables your veterinarian to set up the repayment plan. Ask your vet office if they accept any of these cards as any one of them may be the best way to pay off surprising (and expensive) vet bills. You might also consider a rewards card like the one offered by the American Kennel Club (AKC) that issues three points per dollar spent at pet stores or on AKC purchases.

Joshua Louis Animal Cancer Foundation (JLACF)

Founded by Joshua Louis, the Joshua Louis Animal Cancer Foundation works with Frankie's Friends Partners to help pet owners cover cancer treatment for their pets through grants. To date, this foundation has granted more than $150,000 to families whose pets were in need of expensive cancer-related treatments.

Best Friends

Best Friends is a great resource for pet owners to use to get help paying for medical expenses. In addition to the sources below, Best Friends also provides a state-by-state directory to find financial aid sources for pets in your area. Most of these resources can be explored in a financial aid article at: www.bestfriends.org.

- The Big Hearts Fund: Financial aid for the diagnosis & treatment of dog/cat heart disease
- Brown Dog Foundation: Prescription medications for pets
- Canine Cancer Awareness
- God's Creatures Ministry Veterinary Charity
- IMOM
- Magic Bullet Fund: Cancer-specific
- The Mosby Fund
- The Onyx & Breezy Foundation
- Pets of the Homeless: Pet food and veterinary care assistance for homeless
- The Riedel & Cody Fund: Support for pets suffering with cancer
- RedRover Relief
- Rose's Fund
- Shakespeare Animal Fund

If you're a Patrick Swayze fan, you've probably watched *Roadhouse*. In one scene, a local veterinarian implied Swayze's lifestyle attracted physical altercations. His response was simple, "You can be the kind of person that is looking for trouble, or is ready for it." Being ready for what might happen is what preparation is all about.

Step Two

ATTENTION

CHAPTER 7

We've Got it All Wrong

We've got pet parenting all wrong. Let me illustrate.

You may have heard about the baby elephants that are chained to a steel post anchored in the ground. They try pulling away, but the chain and post are too strong. After a while, they stop trying to pull on the chain and stay in their area. Later, when these same elephants become huge adults, they will stay docile while chained to the same post. Even though these adult elephants could easily pull the post out of the ground or simply break the chain, they don't try to do so, because they are conditioned to believe they can't.

Somewhere along the way, pet owners have become conditioned to thinking that the expert about their pet is their veterinarian. This way of thinking has virtually immobilized pet owners from taking a more active role in their pet's health. In fact, no one knows your pet better than you do. You're the pet expert. Your veterinarian is the medical expert. It takes *both* of you to raise a healthy pet with a longer, more vibrant life. Don't surrender control of your pet's welfare to your veterinarian. Partner with them. To do this effectively, you need preparation of critical documents and supplies (Chapters 1 through 6) and you need to know what to pay attention to that needs extra care so your dog remains happy, healthy and fit. Chapters 7 through 13 of this guide will help you learn what needs your attention.

My staff and I often alert parents to something they've yet to notice: lumps, infected ears, skin irritations, or breathing problems. The response is almost always the same: "How did I miss that lump?" or, "Why didn't I notice that before you did?" The answer is simple: the welfare of their pet is our full-time job so it has our full attention, making it easier for us to notice more subtle changes.

Don't get too dependent on your veterinarian telling you when something is wrong. Most veterinarians only see your pet a few times a year at most. That's too rare to catch many problems in time. Further, you are with your pet more than anyone so raising your awareness of what needs your attention raises the chances of keeping them safe and healthy *all* the time.

This segment of your guide will focus on:

- Attention to Wellness
- Attention to Life Stage
- Attention to Breed
- Attention to Triggers
- Attention to Red Flags
- Attention to Vaccines

Chapter 8

Pay Attention to Your Dog's Overall Health

While the pet owners were vacationing in Las Vegas, I was caring for their two adorable Boston Terriers, Pickles and Peanuts. It was apparent that one of the dogs had some type of gastrointestinal issue because one of them was passing gas that would clear the room. The gas was chronic and so pungent that I had to open doors and use ceiling fans to get rid of the smell. The brothers were practically inseparable, but after two days, I was able to determine the gas source: Pickles. I alerted the parents about the problem in one of my daily video updates that I sent them. Their response was surprising.

"Oh, yeah, we know about Pickle's gas problem," they responded.

"How long has he had such bad gas?" I asked.

"Oh, a really long time."

"Chronic gas like this is not normal," I told the parents.

I wanted permission to talk to their vet to find out if there was something more I should know as well as to explore a change of food. I got the "go ahead" to do both. When I spoke to their veterinarian, she had no idea that Pickles was constantly passing gas, as the parents had never mentioned it during their vet visits. Your vet can't fix what they don't know about.

Pay Attention to Details for Your Vet

Every year you should take your dog to the vet for an annual checkup. This time is usually scheduled for ensuring your dog has updated immunizations (against Parvovirus, Hepatitis, etc.). This is important, but you should also take the time to let your veterinarian conduct a thorough, comprehensive wellness check from nose to tail. Your vet will feel for lumps; move all limbs to find the early onset of joint problems; view teeth and gums to check for dental disease; take notice of your pet's weight; look into ears for cleanliness, mites, and infection; ensure they are well hydrated; check the eyes for cataracts; check stool for parasites; and check blood for any underlying infection. Go to this meeting armed with two things: information and a notebook.

Use the meeting to provide crucial information for your vet. Has your pet's energy or activity level changed? Is their appetite the same? Does your dog walk the same? Are they drinking water normally? It is crucial that you provide anything you've noticed that is a change in their habits or appearance.

Take a notebook with you every time you go to the vet. Make sure the notebook is a folder type with pockets in front or back, or a three-ring binder that you add paper sleeves into to hold documents. This notebook is strictly for your pet. At the annual appointment with your dog's vet, take the checklist below. This should already be in your notebook. Record all information learned from the appointment. This provides you with a complete picture of your dog's overall health. Just as important, the finished document creates a single, definitive summary with benchmarks that serve as measurable guidelines of your pet's wellness. Now, you will have a tool to use from that point on to identify and record critical changes you observe. If you have a pet sitter and other medical specialists for your dog, be sure they get a copy of your pet's annual wellness check.

Pay Attention to Your Dog's Health

I'll be teaching a first aid/CPR class for pet owners and pet caretakers. (Return to Chapter 4 for more details.) During the class, we will discuss something called a snout-to-tail wellness check. Essentially, you sit down with your dog and, with both hands, you slowly feel your way from the snout to the end of the tail. We teach you what to look for in every area of your pet's body: lumps, bumps, flaky skin, and much more. Every dog owner should conduct a snout-to-tail wellness check once a month. To make sure these checks are effective, follow these steps:

One: Use the Wellness Check Form provided on the next page. You can print off a copy from this book or download a free copy from the Pet Parent IQ section at: www.creatureconcierge.com.

Two: Select the right place for this checkup. It should be some place in your home where your pet is comfortable and anticipates something good happening. For example, I have a client who loves his parent's giant, leather ottoman that sits in front of the sofa. The ottoman is where he lays down to gnaw on chew toys and bones. He associates the ottoman with fun, happy times. The ottoman is also firm enough to conduct a wellness check.

Three: Remove any distractions. Turn off your cell phone and television; make sure you pick a time when family and friends are less likely to interrupt you. Don't forget to remove the toys and treats that will distract your dog too.

Four: Take your time. You want to record everything you notice at this stage of your dog's life.

Five: Keep these reports in a handy binder in a convenient location in your home. If you notice anything new before conducting a wellness check the following month, be sure to write it down on the most recent form and don't forget to add the date of the change.

Six: When you go to the vet with your dog, whether for something specific or for an annual checkup, always take your monthly wellness-check forms with you. It is so easy to forget something you've previously noticed or decide not to mention something you think is unimportant (a gassy dog) when in truth it could be a tell-tale sign of something your veterinarian needs to know.

Always remember that recording these important changes in your dog's health is only the first step. *Timely reporting* of these changes to your vet is equally important. If you recently took your dog to the vet, there may be a tendency to wait on notifying your vet of a health change you just noticed about your pet's health. If what you noticed is something that is highly contagious (to other pets or humans) or even the precursor to what could be a critical illness (diabetes or cancer) then communicating these changes should be done immediately, sooner rather than later.

WELLNESS CHECK FOR _____

Date: _____

Head/Body Check

Skin: lumps, lesions, rashes; dry, healthy, flaky. Weight: normal, under, or over?

Notes: _____

Mouth/Teeth

Gums: color, hydration levels. Teeth: plaque levels, breath...

Notes: _____

Ears

Clean, smell-free, hearing normal, excessive scratching...

Notes: _____

Eyes

Vision clarity, weeping, excessive tear staining, cataracts...

Notes: _____

Heart

Heart murmur*, if so what level (1/6, 2/6, 3/6, 4/6, 5/6, 6/6); What treatment is needed as the level of the murmur gets more severe? Heartworms? If so, treatment?

Notes: _____
_____
_____
_____

* Heart murmurs often indicate that Mitral Valve Disease (MVD) is developing. Murmurs are graded on a scale of one to six with one being the least serious to six, the most serious. See Chapter 12 for more details.

Kidneys/Liver

Blood panel results? Functioning at peak?

Notes: _____
_____
_____
_____

Digestive System

Appetite: less, more, normal? Drinking: less, more, normal? Gas?

Notes: _____
_____
_____
_____

Anal Glands/Stool Check

Scooting a lot on their bottom? Condition of waste?

Notes: _____
_____
_____
_____

Nails/Fur (or Hair)

Nails clipped at a healthy length or too long; growing in an inverted way? Is coat shiny or dry?
Excessive shedding? Bald spots?

Notes: _____
_____
_____
_____

Activity:

Is it about the same? Diminished? Does the dog's energy yo-yo up and down?

Notes: _____
_____
_____
_____

Reactions:

To medications? To flea dander? To bee stings? Make sure you note down what allergies, if any, your dog has to any treatment, bite, etc. This info should be on your dog's medical records and on your dog's Emergency Medical Resource Form (see Chapter 2).

Notes: _____
_____
_____
_____

CHAPTER 9

Pay Attention to Your Dog's Life Stage

I grew up with terriers, and I can't help it: I still have a soft spot for them. One West Highland Terrier (Westie) recently in my care was showing signs of joint pain. He was less excited about walking when I picked up his leash, walked much slower, had an awkward gait that clearly demonstrated an unease to place his full weight on his back left hip and leg. It was just another sign that "*Zoro*" had hit another life stage. He had become a senior and was dealing with joint aches and pain. I shared my observations with his mother who got immediate veterinarian care for him so Zoro could enjoy a better quality of life, even at the age of 14.

What is your pet's current life stage? Is your dog a puppy, an adolescent, a young adult, or a mature adult (senior citizen)? What milestones should your dog reach at each stage? What changes should you see? Just like humans, your pet experiences changes to their brain and body at each stage. Understanding what occurs to your dog at each life stage will enable you to make better, proactive decisions that will positively impact their overall health and wellness.

Although your creature kid can't talk, they are *communicating* with you all the time. If you're paying attention, and you know what to look for at each stage, you'll collect the information your pet is *telling* you. It's this information that you and your veterinarian need in order to make prudent decisions about their health and wellness.

What Happens at Each Life Stage?

Before reviewing life-stage specifics, you need to know your dog's age. For many of my readers, it's hard to know their pet's exact age because they adopted an abandoned dog from a rescue group or area animal shelter. Your vet will take a thorough physical examination of your dog's teeth, eyes, joint flexibility, and other tests to help to determine their age. Once you have this estimate, you should next understand their age in dog years.

The old adage that dogs age seven years for every single human year is not very accurate. The American Animal Hospital Association (aaha.org) provides a comprehensive view of a dog's age, based on the size of the dog, on their website. This is a snapshot of the AAHA age chart:

- 3-month-old dog   Equal to five human years
- 1-year-old dog   Equal to 15 human years
- 2-year-old dog   Equal to 24 human years
- Thereafter, add four human years to each additional year so a six-year-old dog would be 40 in human years.

Today the American Veterinary Medical Association (AVMA) uses the guidelines (below) to define the "real" age of a dog. Note: the breed and the size of a dog can also impact how that dog ages. For example, a small or toy breed may not be a "senior" until they are ten years old, whereas a very large breed dog may be a "senior" at six years of age. You can view or order your own 'age' chart from the AVMA or, to see your dog's age by weight/size, go to the Idexx Learning Center age chart.

LIFE STAGES

Now that you know your dog's age, it's important to understand what important 'events' occur at each stage and what you can do to reinforce good behaviors to optimize their health as they age.

PUPPY STAGE

Dog Age: Starts at birth & extends up to about six months of age.
Dog Age in Human Years at this stage: a day old to about 5 years old.

Milestones

Behavior

After the baby is weaned, potty training should begin. This may take up to four to six months. Dogs at this stage want to explore and should be encouraged to experience as many new things as possible: the sound of a dump truck going by, bicycles, Christmas lights, Halloween décor, blenders, etc. This will help build their confidence and minimize fear-based behaviors later in life. Socializing is crucial and should begin around the time your puppy is adopted (about eight weeks) and through their fourth month of life. This teaches them pack behavior (starting with their siblings) and pack hierarchy. Parents need to send a clear message: I am the pack leader and I set the rules. The tone of voice you use when correcting your pup's behavior or the order of who eats in mealtime (you eat your meal and then you feed your pup) are just a few ways to demonstrate you are the leader of the pack.

Food

Should be weaned off their mother's milk around six to eight weeks. Introduce pups to food developed for puppies, as they are still growing and burning fuel faster. Ideally, puppies should be fed four mini meals a day up to three months and three times a day up to six months of age. Note: toy breed puppies may have to be fed four to six small meals a day for up to six months to maintain healthy blood sugar levels. If possible, consider alternatives to traditional hard kibble. See the nutrition section of this book for details.

Health

Pups get their first vaccinations around six to eight weeks of age and will get their last vaccination around week fourteen to sixteen. Most puppies will need to be dewormed. Puppies tend to get Hookworms and/or Roundworms, since the Roundworm larvae (often dormant in the mother) are transmitted to pups via the mother's milk. Their dental health starts early. Puppies have most of their baby teeth at six to eight weeks. Their permanent teeth should be in around seven months.

Parent Action
- Get some help from an experienced (certified) trainer to help with potty training after weaning. You will be shocked at how much easier the process will be when you are taught a few key points. You can often find a trainer in your area through the sources listed in the "Education" section of this book. You may even need to consult with a Board-Certified Veterinary Behaviorist to get help with your dog's behavioral issues.
- Limit your pup's space in the home. This will make it easier to potty train them and keep them in your line of sight.
- During these critical early months, you want to bond with your pup through direct interaction, walks, fetching, and other physical activities like tug of war.
- Get your pup used to your touch with regular hugs and petting. Use downtime, when watching television for example, to rub on the pup's feet, touch the inside and outside of their ears, look at their teeth, and rub their teeth with your fingers. This will make grooming, teeth brushing, and veterinarian exams much easier later on.
- Conduct a cursory dental check at ten weeks (when all baby teeth should already be in) and at ten months (when all adult teeth should be in).
- Make it a point to introduce them to a harness and their first walks on a leash. This is so much easier to do if you leash up and walk another dog with them. If you don't have another dog, ask a friend to bring their dog over so the pup can see you harness up and leash walk another dog. Ideally, walk side by side.
- Last but not least, you must encourage safe socialization from the time their eyes open and they snuggle with siblings up to about their fourteenth week of age. This is a magical window of time where dogs meet other dogs, play with other dogs, and interact with new dogs. Socializing also means exposing your pup/young dog to new sounds and experiences to prevent common noises and equipment from triggering fear or anxiety in the future. Tip: Until your puppy has all their vaccinations, socialization time should be in your home or at a friend's

home/yard with dogs you know are healthy and vaccinated. Avoid dog parks and other large, public areas where your puppy could be exposed to Parvo, Giardia or something else.

ADOLESCENT STAGE
Dog Age: Starts around six months to a year to around two years of age.
Dog Age in Human Years at this stage: about fifteen years to twenty-four years of age.

Milestones

Behavior

Even if you don't have human children, you have likely heard about the terrible twos, when toddlers begin to test the limits of their physical abilities (and the limits of their parents' patience, too). When dogs hit the puberty stage, think of them like a toddler that refuses to grow up. They go from being pups who want to explore to young dogs who want to experiment and … Your well-behaved puppy may suddenly ignore a command they already know or repeat a bad behavior to test your response. Male dogs will often start to mark on trees at this stage; females will begin to mark in popular dog areas to let male dogs know she is available. Your creature kid goes from a small, klutzy puppy to a fast-growing, lanky dog eager to burn energy.

Food

Around six months of age, you can begin to feed your dog two times a day. Some parents continue to serve three meals a day for up to eight months. They should still be eating puppy food to ensure they get the nutrition and calories for fast-growing bodies.

Health

Your puppy will have most of their adult teeth between three to six months of age. You may find a baby tooth on the floor during this time. It is very important to start brushing your pup's teeth as soon as your dog has all his or her adult teeth. Smaller breed dogs will stop growing around six months of age whereas larger breeds' growth spurt slows but may continue growing for nine to twelve to fifteen months. If you have not spayed or neutered your dog, this is the time you should talk to your vet about doing so.

Parent Action
- Work with a trainer to teach your young, active dog four critical commands: sit, stay, leave it, and drop it. Be patient. Your dog, at this stage, will often have the attention span of a gnat. Keep lessons down to ten to fifteen minutes on each training element.
- Remember your dog is a pack animal. They need a few hours of socializing time with other dogs and humans, daily. Socialization with other dogs teaches your dog how to read other dogs' behaviors, how to interact when playing, and helps them realize dogs (not just humans) can be a great source of joy and companionship.
- Now that your pup is acting more like a toddler, it's important to puppy-proof your home. Not only will your dog become very active, they will also pick up and swallow virtually anything. Look behind and under all furniture to make sure there are no small items available for a dog to swallow. I did this with a family who adopted a nine-month-old pup. We found a pen cap, water bottle lid, a rubber band, a hook used to hang Christmas decorations on a tree, and a child's sock. Any one of these items could have been disastrous if swallowed by a dog.
- Kitchen: make sure all sharp items (knives, scissors) are put away every time so you won't accidentally knock them off a counter and into a dog's eyes.
- Remove all toys (human and canine) that are not in good condition.
- Cords: young dogs will often chew or pull on electrical cords. Cover them with cord covers, block with furniture or doggie gates. Block dogs from getting under beds and sofas where they can access cords. This can be done with a variety of products, including the Upstone Gap Bumper and the BowerBird Under the bed barrier.

Pay Attention to Your Dog's Life Stage

- Your 'toddler' will test boundaries and your patience by ignoring commands they know and/or repeating behaviors you've taught them to avoid. Be consistent with your commands and praise so you don't confuse your dog. Make sure all family members use the same commands, praise and rewards process.
- Male dogs, coming into puberty will start to display their manliness by marking frequently on bushes, trees, and anything vertical. Females will pee more often to communicate her availability as she comes into heat for the first time. As 1.5 million shelter animals are still euthanized in America each year, (670,000 dogs, 860,000 cats) please set up an appointment to have your dog spayed or neutered. Talk to your vet about the health benefits aligned with spaying and neutering.
- Your pup will grow a lot during this stage. Check collars and harnesses to make sure they still fit properly and haven't become too tight.
- Make sure, if you have multiple people in the home, that everyone is consistent with what they allow your dog to do or not do. I repeat: clear, consistent expectations are critical for your dog.
- Be patient. As mentioned previously, your dog, at this stage, will often have the attention span of a gnat.

ADULT STAGE

Dog Age: starts at about three years of age to about the age of six. Dog Age in Human Years at this stage: about twenty-eight years to forty-two years of age.

Milestones

Behavior

Think about your dog's age (in human years) at this point. They will go from puppy to teenager (around fifteen years of age) to young adult (twenty-nine years of age). Think about how much you changed during that time. Your dog will go from a hyper puppy to a less active grown up. They will be more inclined to nap than take another walk. One of the most frustrating issues for parents at this stage is that they often have to deal with their grown dog getting upset over the same triggers they had as pups. If your dog was terrified of storms as a puppy, and you didn't work through those fears then, your grown dog is likely to still be afraid of storms.

Food
Watch your dog's weight at this stage. Make sure they are off puppy food and eating two, not three, meals of adult dog food a day. Be careful to measure what they get (so they don't overeat but are still getting enough to fuel their active bodies). If you have more than one dog, make sure they all eat in separate areas to ensure no one is overeating.

Health
Note that during this time, your dog's teeth will begin to show a little wear and may begin to yellow. You may see broken teeth or receding gums. Make sure a thorough dental checkup is done every year when your pet gets a veterinarian wellness check.

Parent Action
- Keep your dog's mind engaged and sharp with interactive toys, walking in new areas, and serving food in puzzle containers.
- Use the commands your dog learned as a puppy to ensure they continue to respond to them quickly.
- If your dog is food-motivated, be sure to use a low-fat/low-calorie treat when you reward them.

SENIOR STAGE
Dog Age: As early as seven years of age.
Dog Age in Human Years: about forty-seven years of age.

Milestones

Behavior
You may notice your dog trips on a sidewalk, or misses the step off the curb once in a while. Your dog likely wants slower (and fewer) walks and may gray around their muzzle and head. You have a senior citizen on your hands, and their eyesight is not as sharp. Slow their walking

pace a bit and, if you are walking on a new path/new area, give them time to adapt to the terrain. Over time, you may see your dog appear more sensitive, even stressed with the simplest changes to your routine and their routine. Try to be consistent. If you have slick floors, it is much easier for seniors to fall, and they are often slower to get up. You may notice them pulling a leg or limping a bit at this age. Your dog may begin to suffer from arthritic pain. They may be less enthusiastic about walking or retreat more to a quiet place. Be alert to cognitive changes as your pet may show signs of dementia or something more debilitating: canine cognitive dysfunction (CCD).

Food

As their joints age, every pound your dog weighs over their ideal weight places great undue pressure on joints that can eventually falter. Most dogs walk less now, so make sure they eat food designed for their age that will also help them maintain a healthy size.

Health

As your older pup's eyesight and hearing are compromised, they may not hear what you say or see hand commands and end up hurt. I remember when my little dog Shasta's eyesight was changing. One evening, we raced across the street to chase a rabbit at dusk, and she failed to see the edge of the curb in time and tripped. Be conscious of your dog's abilities as they age, particularly as it relates to their safety when you take them to dog parks or other people's homes/yards. Your dog's teeth are also more fragile at this time. They will tend to show more tartar, some yellowing, and wear. See the Chronic Bad Breath section in Chapter 12 for more details on dental care.

Parent Action

- Consider purchasing inexpensive runners from discount retailers (Walmart or Target) to place in the most common areas where your dog walks in the house. These will give him a no-slip grip and make it easier to get up, too.
- Switch out that cute round bed for a comfy, orthopedic bed at home. If you crate them, place an orthopedic bed in their crate too.

- Avoid surprising your dog, as this can be more stressful at this age.
- Provide ramps for larger dogs to make it easier to get into and out of vehicles.
- Change how they exercise. My 10-pound dog, Nokona, began to avoid walking at all, making it easy to gain weight. I purchased a doggie swimming pool deep enough for him to swim off calories without placing stress on his older joints. Note: he wears a life jacket when swimming.
- Talk to your vet about joint supplements to help lubricate their older joints. New medicines and medical procedures are created all the time. When Adequan came out, it was a game changer for some dogs with degenerative or traumatic arthritis. Ask your veterinarian what's available to ease the discomfort of arthritic pain as well as what treatments could improve joint movement. Make the senior years comfortable and enjoyable.

A great source of life stage information can be found on the American Animal Hospital Association website. This informative site also includes a Canine Life Stage Calculator that enables dog owners to view a personalized age specific, life stage summary for their dog.

See the Education, section five of this book, for a link to the calculator.

Chapter 10

Pay Attention to Your Dog's Breed

Humans, by the thousands, are getting DNA tests to discover their fascinating genetic history. I've done this myself and was surprised to discover I am 27 percent Irish (who'da thought?) and even have a smidgeon of Inuit in my bloodline. It's just as fun and fascinating to do this for your pet. It's also very smart to know your creature kid's genetic make-up. Why?

Some breeds are genetically predisposed to certain behaviors and others to certain health issues. Knowing what your dog's DNA make-up is can reveal some very important information. Specifically, identify breed behavioral tendencies which:

- Helps adopters to decide if a particular dog is a good fit for their family, their lifestyle, and their geographic area
- Make it easier to motivate and train your dog to overcome training challenges
- Identify predisposed health conditions to pre-emptively minimize the impact on your pet's health

Although your dog's genetics are not an absolute predictor for breed-related health issues, genetics can shine a light on what should have your attention to help you anticipate and prepare for potential health-related challenges. Case in point: let's say your dog's DNA results indicate they are primarily Cocker Spaniel. Cockers tend to have chronic ear infections. Some Cockers struggle with so many ear infections that they end up with something called cauliflower ear that often requires serious (and expensive) ear surgery. Knowing this in advance, you can save your money, and your Cocker discomfort and pain, by taking certain steps. First, learn how to clean their ears at home. Hire a groomer with the skills to ensure ears are washed while limiting water entering the ear canal. Make sure the hair inside the ear area is kept to a minimum to reduce the heat that often contributes to yeast infections in the ear. In this way, your knowledge of your dog's DNA helps diminish the impact of breed-related health issues on their life and your wallet.

There are some dog breeds prone to obesity, including Labrador Retrievers, Basset Hounds, Dachshunds, Beagles, and Scottish Terriers. If your dog's DNA indicates their dominant breed is one prone to obesity, you know up front they will need more exercise and/or careful management of what they eat.

There are other revelations that come to light with DNA testing that have more serious implications—one of which is identifying genetic mutations. One to note is the Multidrug resistance-1 (MDR1) gene mutation. A dog with MDR1 cannot process drugs out of the brain. Without the ability to remove certain drugs from their brain, they can build up to toxic levels. This can cause blindness, disorientation, tremors, seizures, and even death.

In regards to training, DNA information can be invaluable. Each breed group has distinctive behavioral characteristics. Which breed group is your dog in: the herding group, the hound group, the non-sporting group, the terrier group, the toy group, or the working group? Let's say you had a DNA test that reveals your new rescue dog is predominantly a flat-coated retriever. This retriever is from the sporting group and will likely need a lot of activity. You would need to be sure he gets vigorous exercise. If you're a runner, he will make a great running companion. If not, you will need to explore other activities like doggie daycare, fetching, or maybe agility course training. Fulfilling their need for interaction (emphasis on *action*), this retriever will make a great companion; without it, the breed can get frustrated and even destructive.

Have Your Dog Take a DNA test

Even the best of us may not correctly guess our dog's breed. In fact, according to veterinary geneticist Angela Hughes, D.F.M., Ph.D, few can. Hughes notes, "Most people can guess just one breed present in a mixed-breed dog less than 25 percent of the time." Whether a purebred, a mixed breed or a designer pet (a mix of two purebreds) it is easier to train your dog, care for your dog, and take preventative measures that protect your dog\'s health and wellness if you know their breed(s).

DNA testing for dogs and cats is available from a multitude of companies. A few of the more popular are listed below. The cost for pet genetic testing varies from fifty to one hundred dollars. Not all deliver the information you may need or want. When choosing a test, make sure the company's breed comparison database is large. Also determine if they provide ancillary information, like reports on health-related issues/diseases, training tips, and the ability to identify both paternal and maternal ancestry. I prefer the Wisdom Health Panel because of its comprehensive results. Wisdom testing results include detailed breed data, trace ancestry back to their great grandparents, screen for medical conditions, and more. Go to jetpetDNA at www.creatureconcierge.com to purchase a DNA testing kit for your dog from our preferred testing company.

DNA testing kit companies to consider:

- DNA My Dog Test
- Embark Dog DNA Test
- Find My Pet DNA
- Wisdom Health Panel

Once you know your pet's breed, use that knowledge to pay attention to what your pet really needs to maintain a healthy, lively, long life. Be more conscious of your dog's DNA-related needs at each stage of life.

CHAPTER 11

Pay Attention to Your Dog's Triggers

One day, I was walking an adorable (and feisty) little female Shih Tzu named Raza. The weather was nice and all seemed fine. Suddenly a dog, walking with his parents on the opposite side of the street, barked loudly and lunged forward. His parent lost him, and the dog and leash came charging our way. He was small, but I learned even a small dog can bite. I picked up Raza, grabbed her leash, and turned away from the loose dog until his owner could run across the street and grab him. He was not neutered, and Raza had triggered his mating tendencies.

What are Common Triggers for Dogs?

What are triggers? They are any event, physical item, sound, or smell that triggers extreme fear, anxiety, or reactive behavior in your pet. In the most extreme form, a former active combat military dog's trigger might be to run for cover under a bed when they hear a car backfire. In a less extreme form, your dog may tremble violently and drool excessively during storms with extreme thunder and lightning. Triggers can also incite aggressive behavior. For example, a puppy once punished with a broom may attack all brooms when he becomes an adult.

What follows is a short list of typical triggers:

Sounds: lightning, thunder, fireworks, leaf blowers, mowers, vacuum cleaners...

Machines: tractors, construction equipment...

Vehicles: backfiring, loud/large waste trucks, busses...

Metal: ladders, bicycles...

Strangers: humans, other dogs they don't know...

Décor: Halloween, Christmas decorations, flags...

Why is it so important to know what your dog's triggers are at every life stage? For one, triggers can cause knee-jerk reactions that could get them killed. Let me explain.

The dog that came after Raza escaped from his home, backyard, and owner's hands at least seven times (that I know of) as a reaction to his trigger: the need to mate. We encourage parents to have their dogs spayed and neutered. Male dogs are especially driven by the urge to mate and are quick to run to any opportunity. It should be noted that statistically, the odds are not in their favor for surviving this urge, as vehicles kill six million dogs every year. Eighty-five percent of those dogs hit by vehicles are unaltered males.

There are triggers that incite some dogs to attack other dogs. Training, for the dog owner (not just the dog) is paramount in these situations; training would include how to recognize the dog's triggers and how to head them off.

Secondly, triggers can often cause your dog to feel anxiety. In its lightest form, the anxiety may just manifest itself as cowering in a corner until the trigger passes. In extreme cases, your dog may pant excessively, whimper, pace repeatedly, and drool. This kind of extreme stress, too often, can cause serious health issues.

Thirdly, triggers can also cause destructive behavior. One precious dog that I care for periodically literally becomes unhinged when her humans leave her alone. Dogs like this, regardless of their size, may destroy dog beds, furniture, trash, and anything else they can access.

Does your pet have triggers? If so, do you know what they are? Have they changed over time? How can these seemingly innocuous, inanimate objects and events terrify your dog or signal a dangerous reaction? What do you do about them to help your dog maintain a relaxed state regardless of the triggers? It's a challenge, especially if you have a rescue dog that may have survived a traumatic event that they can't explain. With training (and, in certain situations, with medication), your dog can improve their coping skills and minimize their trigger-reactive nature.

Action:

- Make note of your dog's triggers. Be sure to identify the trigger, when it happened (date/time), and how your dog reacted.
- Next, work with your dog to eliminate his reactive instincts to the trigger. When my dog Nokona was a puppy, he jumped out of his skin the first time he saw a giant black trash bag on the sidewalk. I paused, let him relax, and then knelt down near the bag and I touched the bag. I talked happy talk to Nokona while I stroked the bag. Seeing how calm I was around the bag, Nokona's curiosity got the better of him. I let him take his time. He slowly came over to the bag to sniff it, and then touched it with his nose. He was never afraid of a garbage bag again. Remember, your dog picks up on your energy so it is important not to project angst around your dog's triggers. Stay calm, confident, and quiet.
- Should your dog's trigger cause more extreme behavior you can't seem to help him or her conquer, consider reaching out to a dog trainer for help. Most of the time, you can receive the direction and information to help your dog work through the fears that accompany their triggers or diminish the reactive nature they create. A skilled trainer will also provide you with the parenting skills so you can help your pup exhibit trigger-free behavior.
- Share these details with your veterinarian. In extreme cases, consider taking your dog to a Board Certified Veterinarian Behaviorist who is trained and licensed to diagnose and treat both medical and behavioral problems with animals.

What are your dog's triggers?

CHAPTER 12

Pay Attention to Your Dog's Red Flags

Sometimes it's easier for me to get parents to relate to their pet's needs if I relate a situation to people first. Are you one of those humans that looked down at the scales one day only to see you had somehow put on four pounds? It wasn't good to see the scales go up, but you thought to yourself, "No worries, I can easily shed a few pounds." Fast-forward to a year later and you realize that four pounds has turned into eleven pounds. Your doctor talks to you about getting more exercise when she finishes your annual physical. You nod your head, affirming you'll add that task to your daily to-do list. By Thanksgiving the following year, as you shop for larger clothes, you wonder how you gained so much weight so fast. You didn't. They were coming on board your body little by little. You just weren't paying attention until those pounds began to make it difficult to climb stairs, made your knees ache on walks, and contributed to your high blood pressure.

Our pets' health changes happen in a similar fashion; they are usually subtler, more incremental. So much so, we don't notice them until the subtle changes are signs of a serious health condition. In a 2007 Veterinary Economics article entitled *Seeing Double*, M. Rehm noted, "… that at least 10% of pets that appear healthy to their owners and their veterinarians during annual checkups have underlying diseases." Yikes!

Most domestic animals (dogs, cats, ferrets, rabbits) will hide any indicators of illness or injury for as long as possible. It is their genetic prey-versus-predator instinct kicking in. Their perception is that outwardly demonstrating that they don't feel good or are hurting makes them vulnerable to be left behind or eaten by a predator. Your pet may *pretend* to enjoy their walks, playtime, tug of war, or the introduction of a new toy while inside they feel pain.

"Red flags" are like little alarms waving in the wind, trying to get our attention. One of the reasons we encourage parents to maintain a wellness check every month is that it makes it easier to catch these signs of health distress early on and give them the attention they need before it's too late.

Red Flags to Watch For

Excessive Drinking/Urination

Is your dog suddenly drinking a lot more water? How are you measuring their water intake to be sure? Are they drinking more often? Is your dog going to other sources of water (the tub, shower) seeking more opportunities to drink? Excessive drinking could be a red flag message: my pet is borderline diabetic. Drinking significantly less water could be a red flag message: my dog is sick.

Blood in Urine, Struggling to Urinate

Is that a slight pink tint to your dog's urine? Is your pet struggling to urinate? It may be early signs of a urinary tract infection (UTI) or even bladder stones.

Chronic Bad Breath

You just had your dog's teeth cleaned by your vet. They only had to pull two teeth and the others look white and shiny. So why, only a week later do you notice your dog has terrible breath again? Chronic bad breath is not normal for a dog. Work with a vet and nutritionist to determine if their bad breath is a sign of dental disease you can't see or an indication of problems in the digestive system. To be clear, the smell in the mouth can be generated from problems in the stomach. Sometimes a change to a healthier diet is all that is needed. See the Nutrition section of this guide, starting in Chapter 21 for more insight about food and its contribution to a healthier digestive system.

Excessive Gas/Stool Changes

Does your pet have gas that could clear a room? Have you noticed your dog's stool is inconsistent or poorly formed? Is there a jelly-like goop around it? This may be a red flag that your dog or cat has food sensitivities, food allergies, or colitis.

Noticeable Activity Change

Your dog no longer eagerly jumps into your truck. He also appears to struggle getting up after an overnight sleep and limps a little after first getting up from a nap. No longer jumping off or on their favorite spot could be a red flag that your dog is now struggling with joint or spinal pain. It could also be a signal that your pet's depth perception is now more compromised so they lack the confidence to jump to certain heights. These slight changes may be arthritic pain, an indication their eyesight is failing, or a hint your dog is suffering from Lyme disease that can also cause aches in joints.

Excessively Licking Paws

You're petting your dog one evening when you see his paws look darker, stained. Watch to see if your pet is constantly licking their paws. This may be a red flag: allergies.

Chronic Ear Scratching

What is that smell? Are your dog's ears a source of a mucky, yeasty smell? When did your dog start scratching her ears so much? Your dog may have the onset of a yeast or bacteria infection in his or her ears; your dog may have ear mites.

Doggie Dandruff

What is that bald spot on your dog's back? Are there more? Is it your imagination, or is your dog shedding a lot more this summer? It may be that your dog simply needs Omega 3 fatty acids added to their diet to improve the health of their skin and coat. On the other hand, it could be those hot spots are a bacterial infection, flea dander, dermatitis, ringworm, or a hint your dog is battling parasites of some kind. On the other hand, bald spots and dry hair along with excessive shedding and chronic lethargy could be an indication that your dog is suffering from hypothyroidism.

Vomiting

You've likely seen your dog throw up everything from bile to hairballs. This is not likely to be cause for concern. However, if there is blood or funky (my oh-so *technical* description) brownish grains in their vomit, it could be a sign that your pet swallowed an object that is irritating the stomach.

Heart Murmurs

As the mitral valve of your dog's heart degenerates (mitral valve disease or MVD), it results in an irregular flow often referred to as a heart murmur. If your dog is diagnosed with a heart murmur, work with your veterinarian to understand the stage of the murmur (one is low; six is advanced) and what treatment is available. Dr. Kate Meurs, a faculty member at North Carolina State College of Veterinary Medicine, specializes in MVD genetics. She notes, "[MVD] accounts for a whopping 75 percent of all heart problems diagnosed by veterinarians – that's more than all other heart diseases, in both cats and dogs, combined.

Significant Appetite Change

Is your dog a picky eater that just doesn't like her food very much, or did you notice she's eating less? Always measure out what you feed your pet so you know what they are eating. The same goes with water. If you have cats and dogs, be sure to note changes can be very different for them. If a dog stops eating for a day or so, he may have a slight upset tummy or is simply hoping you will accidentally drop something off the dinner table into his mouth.

This is another reason I encourage parents to measure their pet's food and water. It's an easy method of recognizing something is off. Are they eating less each day or suddenly acting picky about the food you serve them? You won't know if you're not paying attention to the quantity they eat.

Pay Attention to Your Dog's Red Flags

Paying attention to triggers is not about becoming paranoid regarding your dog's behavior or fitness. Nor are they about self-diagnosing your dog. (Speak to your vet, not Dr. Google.) Instead, timely recognition of red flags are a simple way of preemptively *recording, reporting, and reacting* to changes going on with your pet in time for your veterinarian to help you address them and avoid more serious health conditions. In fact, some of those annoying tests your veterinarian wants to run (and you think are a waste of your money) are often designed for early detection of diseases. I want to reinforce this point to all dog owners: Veterinarians do not receive a crystal ball along with a diploma when they graduate. Blood panels, X-rays, fecal tests, ear cytology evaluations are just a few methods your veterinarian can use to determine what is impacting your dog's health. Further, testing can often diagnose a health issue before you know it exists and also guide your veterinarian on what treatment is best for your dog.

Set up a system to give these red flags your attention. I conduct my pet's wellness check on the same day I give him his monthly flea/tick treatment on the 25th of every month. Part of the wellness check is evaluating how he is doing with old triggers. One of my clients has her alarm set to celebrate her dog's birthday every month. Her phone alarm, tied to her phone calendar, goes off on the 6th of every month (her dog was born on July 6). The alarm reminds her to treat for fleas, ticks, and to conduct a wellness check, too.

CHAPTER 13

Pay Attention to Your Dog's Treatments

It was the kind of phone call you don't want to get. My client's dog was near death. She asked for prayers and a consoling ear. "What happened?" I asked. Apparently her dog had an extreme, adverse reaction to a vaccine for Leptospirosis and now he's on the verge of kidney failure.

There are core vaccines (required) and noncore vaccines (suggested). The Leptospirosis vaccine is optional (suggested) and can have some serious adverse effects. Whereas core vaccinations are for highly contagious, common, and deadly viruses, non-core vaccinations should be evaluated based on your routine, lifestyle, and geographic location. For example, if you live in a state where mosquitoes, fleas, and ticks are more prevalent, it would be prudent to make sure your dog is on flea, tick, and heartworm treatment year round.

Knowing the fundamentals about core and noncore vaccines will help you make the best decisions for your dog. Work with your vet.

Dog Immunizations: Recommended & Required

Bordetella (Also known as Kennel Cough)

NonCore

Form: Nasal spray. (There is an injectable available.)

Purpose: This vaccine is for a highly infectious bacterium that is also the primary cause of kennel cough. NOTE: A dog can also get Kennel Cough from a virus like parainfluenza.

Signs: Severe coughing, vomiting.

Transmission:	By inhaling bacteria particles that another (infected) dog (or cat) sneezes or coughs out. Can also contract by directly licking or nuzzling an infected dog.
Required:	Most boarding and daycare facilities require it. If your dog goes to dog parks and/or plays with friends' dogs, it is also recommended, as this bacteria is so infectious.

Distemper

Core

Form:	Injectable
Purpose:	This vaccine is designed to support the dog's overall system and prevent secondary infections against this highly infectious virus. There is no cure.
Signs:	Fever, coughing, vomiting, seizures, twitching, diarrhea, paralysis, death.
Transmission:	From infected dog's eye or nose secretions; from their urine or feces. It can be airborne or transferred from objects like blankets.
Required:	There is no law requiring this vaccine but the disease is easily transmitted, so it is highly recommended. Most daycare and boarding facilities require it.

Hepatitis

Core

Form:	Injectable
Purpose:	Also referred to as Adenovirus, this vaccine boosts a dog's ability to fight the symptoms as opposed to serving as a cure.
Signs:	Range from low fever, congestion, vomiting, jaundice, pain around the liver, stomach enlargement.
Transmission:	Infected dogs can transmit hepatitis to other dogs via their urine, stool, saliva, blood, nasal discharge. Note: A dog that recovers from Hepatitis remains infective up to nine months.
Required:	This virus is very contagious and affects multiple organs (liver, kidneys, spleen, lungs, and eyes) so it is

highly recommended. Many daycare/boarding facilities require it.

Leptospirosis (Lepto)

NonCore

Form:	Injectable. Antibiotics to fight this disease caused when a dog is infected by the Leptospira (bacterial organism).
Purpose:	The treatment is designed to fight off bacterial infection. Like Rabies, Lepto is a zoonotic disease that can also spread from dog to human.
Signs:	Fever, vomiting, loss of appetite, diarrhea, lethargy, muscle and abdominal pain, increased thirst, urinating more often. In more extreme situations, a dog may have a tarry poop, an irregular pulse, enlarged lymph nodes.
Transmission:	It's ingested when a dog drinks stagnant water contaminated with the bacterium. Contamination occurs when a wild animal (rats, mice, raccoons, feral cats, skunks) carrying the bacterium urinates in the water. Dogs can also get Lepto when they swim in contaminated ponds where they can easily ingest the water or when they lick their paws after stepping on a contaminated surface.
Required:	No, but recommended as it can cause liver and kidney failure, and if treatment starts too late, or the dog is at a more vulnerable stage of life, it can be fatal. NOTE: You might consider having it administered at a separate time from other vaccines to minimize the side effects.

Parainfluenza

NonCore

Form:	Injectable. Often part of a dog's annual vaccine series along with Bordetella
Purpose:	To fight a virus that contributes to kennel cough.

Signs:	Nasal discharge, sneezing, fever, coughing, loss of appetite, eye inflammation.
Transmission:	Dog to dog through sneezing, coughing, shared water, food.
Required:	No, but easily transmitted so highly recommended.

Parvovirus

Core

Form:	Injectable.
Purpose:	Help dogs fight the impact (extreme diarrhea, dehydration) of this deadly, and highly contagious virus.
Signs:	Attacks the gastrointestinal system so a dog loses his or her appetite and experiences extreme vomiting as well as fever and bloody diarrhea.
Transmission:	When a dog has direct contact with an infected dog or makes contact with an infected dog's feces.
Required:	Both puppies and unvaccinated dogs can easily contract and die from this virus so it is highly recommended to get the vaccine.

Rabies

Core

Form:	Injectable vaccine.
Purpose:	Prevents contracting this disease.
Signs:	Rabies attacks a dog's central nervous system. Infected dogs will experience extreme headaches, hallucinations, irrational anxiety, paralysis, and eventually death.
Transmission:	Through the bite or a scratch from an infected animal.
Required:	Yes. All US states require dogs be vaccinated against rabies. Note: rabies can also be contracted by humans.

Additional Dog Treatments: Often Recommended

Heartworm Prevention

Dogs contract heartworms through the bite of an infected female mosquito that deposits larvae through repeated bites to the host (dog). Once the larvae mature (about sixty days later) the adult worms will travel to the heart and lungs. If not treated, the worms keep growing, making it difficult for the dog to breathe and eventually, they will kill the dog. Want to save money? Treating a dog with heartworms is up to twenty-five times more expensive than prevention. Solution: give your dog a monthly heartworm-prevention chewable pill. One of my favorite treatments is ProHeart® 6, an injection that your dog only needs twice a year. Note: ProHeart® 12, now available, makes it possible for your dog to get one injection each year. Although mosquitoes rely on sugar as their primary source of energy, they feed on (human and animal) blood to fertilize their eggs. By using a treatment to repel mosquitoes, they will not fall victim to heartworms.

Flea Prevention

Fleas can carry and transmit tapeworms and can cause flea allergy Dermatitis and anemia. Fleas can also carry and transmit (to humans) typhus, plague, spotted fever and cat scratch fever. Dogs bitten by fleas often suffer extreme allergic reactions to flea dander, scratching incessantly until their skin shows. They are also at risk of contracting these deadly diseases. These nasty parasites live all over the U.S. They are attracted to your dog's body heat. Even dogs that primarily live indoors will find themselves victim to fleas. Once they bite your dog, they produce eggs that drop to the ground, living on your floors and in your carpet until they hatch. Treatments fall into three categories:

Collars: like Seresto®
Topical: like Advantage® II (for dogs), Frontline® Plus, Frontline® Gold, K9 Advantix® II, Effitix®, Fifproguard®)
Oral: like Comfortis®, Capstar®, Advantus®

Tick Prevention

Ticks can transmit Lyme disease or Rocky Mountain spotted fever. Both dogs and humans can contract these diseases from a tick bite. Treatments come in different forms, including sprays, powders, collars, shampoos, dips, and pills.

Collars: like Seresto®

Topical: like Advantage® II (for dogs), Frontline® Plus, Frontline® Gold, Revolution®, K9 Advantix® II, Effitix®, Fiproguard®, Vectra 3D®)

Oral: like Comfortis®

Multi-Treatment Options and Organics:

Explore your options. Some treatments prevent multiple conditions. See options below. Review the merits and adverse effects of each product.

- Simparica Trio ®: Protects against fleas, ticks, and some parasites
- Nexgard®: Protects against fleas, ticks, and some parasites
- Simparica® Trio: Prevents heartworm disease and protects against ticks, fleas, roundworms, and hookworms
- Trifexis®: Protects against fleas, adult hookworms, whipworms, roundworms, and prevents heartworm disease
- K9 Advantix® II: Protects against fleas, flea eggs, ticks, and prevents heartworm disease
- Effitix®: Protects against fleas, ticks, chewing lice, and prevents heartworm disease
- Vetra 3D®: Protects against fleas, ticks, chewing lice, and prevents heartworm disease

High-Risk Dogs, Alternative Treatments

Some of our Creature Concierge clients (dogs) are fragile. They may be immunocompromised or they are at a hospice-care stage of life. Some immunizations, as well as flea, tick, or heartworm treatments may be too harsh for them. Or, they may be allergic to some of these treatments. If so, consider organic alternatives. Dr. Karen Becker, who practices both traditional and natural veterinary methods, recommends Dr. Mercola® Flea and Tick Defense, an essential oil product. Dogs prone to seizures should not take oral flea and tick medicine. There are some topical treatments that can be used to treat these dogs, but consult with your veterinarian before you choose one.

Medications

Next, I'll provide a list of the typical vaccinations administered at each stage of your dog's life. Before doing so, I want to pause to provide my readers with a "WATCH IT" alert regarding general medications. When your veterinarian prescribes a new medication, ask about that treatment's side effects. Apoquel® is a very effective treatment for allergy-driven itching. Having said that, it may also cause parasitic skin infections or pre-existing cancers to get worse.

Tip: Read the small print and the "important safety information" portion of the medication pamphlet provided with all treatments. It can also be helpful to read independent, long-term studies of a new medication.

Typical Vaccination Time Table

Puppies

6-8 Weeks Old	Distemper, Adenovirus (Hepatitis), Parvovirus (all three are called DAP)
10-12 Weeks Old	DAP (second round)
12-14 Weeks Old	Rabies
14-16 Weeks Old	DAP (third and final round)

Young Adults

12-16 months	Rabies and DAPP (adding parainfluenza)
Annually	DAPP

Mature Adults

Every three years	Rabies (also comes in one-year doses)
Annually	DAPP

Seniors

Every three years	Rabies (also comes in one-year doses)
Annually	DAPP

Remember, you don't need to be an expert to take better care of your dog. However, to ensure your dog has optimum health, you do have to be his or her greatest advocate. To that end, it is imperative you understand why your vet recommends certain vaccines and treatments, the impact they have on your dog's well-being, and the potential adverse outcomes they may have on your dog. Don't be afraid to ask your veterinarian questions; below are some I recommend. Take this guide with you and record your vet's answers so you can use their helpful information at all stages of your dog's life.

Questions to Ask; Issues to Consider:

- Does my dog really need all the DAPP vaccines every year? Can the vaccines be separated to give one at a time rather than one vaccine all at once?
- Can my dog build up immunities so they can get fewer vaccines?
- What is the difference between DAPP and DHPP?
- What side effects accompany each immunization? Will an allergy pill or steroid shot, administered before the vaccines, minimize the side effects?
- I've heard the Titer test can be used to measure my dog's immunity for most diseases. Is this true? If the Titer test proves my dog has antibodies (from previous vaccinations), can I avoid giving my dog so many vaccinations?
- Can any of the vaccines pose a threat to my dog's life? If yes, which ones? If so, why would I give it to my dog?
- I'm trying to take advantage of the early months of my puppy's life to get them socialized. How early can I give him/her the Bordetella vaccine so he can play with other dogs?
- Is it okay for my dog to play with other dogs before he has received all his vaccines?
- What non-core treatments are critical for my dog? Why?
- Are there vaccines that have adverse effects if my dog is taking certain supplements? If my dog is taking certain prescription drugs?

If my dog is about to have surgery? If my dog is sick? If my dog has seizures? If my dog's autoimmune system is compromised?
- Will you be giving the vaccinations in different areas (hip, neck, leg)? Why or why not?
- Now that my dog is older and more fragile, does he/she still need all the vaccines?
- I have cats and dogs. Is there any vaccine or flea/tick treatment that I might give my dog that could hurt my cat and visa versa? (Hint: The answer is yes.)
- Should I give vaccines at different times? Will the adverse effects of vaccines be diminished if they are given to my dog several weeks apart?
  - Note: If your dog reacts to a treatment, this information should be written in your dog's file and on your dog's Emergency Medical Resource Form. Record your dog's vaccination site (right side of neck, back left hip), date, time of day, and brand of the vaccine or treatment he reacted to for future reference.
- Should bacterial vaccines be given at the same time as viral vaccines?
- My dog is still nursing her puppies. Can she get vaccinations during this time?
- If my dog responds poorly to a vaccine, how will that look to me? What reactions should warrant taking him to my vet or a pet emergency hospital?
- Does the company that produces these vaccines and treatments provide an information sheet to describe how it works and possible side effects? Tip: These products almost always have Client Information Sheets about their products online, but many veterinarians also carry these in their vet offices. Ask for them and *read* them prior to choosing a medication.

- Does an "all in one" parasite treatment cover all fleas, ticks, and heartworm? For example, Trifexis is often referred to as an "all in one" protection product for most parasites. You would be shocked at how many parents assume then that this is for fleas and ticks. It isn't. Trifexis doesn't protect your dog against ticks. Further, some of the products that protect against multiple parasites cause more side effects. Take the time to read up on these treatments and talk to your vet about the most effective and safe option.

Step Three

PREVENTION

CHAPTER 14

Why Didn't You Tell Me?

I can't explain it, but we care for numerous dogs that are enamored with eating acorns. I guess the squirrels know something we don't. One of my tinier clients was an enthusiastic acorn eater. His parents took extreme measures to keep him from ingesting acorns. Despite this, it was acorns that contributed to kidney failure and ultimately his death.

Acorns can be toxic to dogs. They contain tannins that cause stomach distress and diarrhea. Too many acorns can lead to internal damage and abdominal obstruction; to kidney failure that can be fatal.

The truth is that too many of the vet visits you will make (especially the more expensive ones) are to deal with injuries, incidents, or illnesses that can often be prevented. This segment will focus on the most common preventable injuries and illnesses.

This segment of your guide will focus on preventing:
- In-Home Accidents
- Outdoor Accidents
- Off-Site Accidents
- Activity-Related Accidents
- Poison Incidents
- Dental Disease
- Obesity

CHAPTER 15

Prevent Accidents At Home

I picked up my ringing phone and noticed a neighbor's name displayed on the screen. The last time Vicki and I had spoken, her dog had gotten out of the house. With a little help from some landscaping workers, I found her dog a few days later. Unfortunately, it was too late; a car had hit him.

"Jet," she said, "My (new) dog got out. My roommate wasn't paying attention, and when she opened the front door to leave for work, he got out."

I quickly walked through the checklist of pet-rescue steps to take in order to get her dog home quickly. I could write a mini book on how to find a lost dog but some of the immediate steps I had Vicki take: make a flier with a photo of your dog, your contact info, where the dog was last seen/when last seen, and a description of your dog. Circulate this with your local animal control, area veterinarians, online neighborhood groups like Next Door, and on prominent intersections in nearby neighborhoods. Take a few of your (dirty) clothes and place near the entrance of your garage door. Raise your garage door to give your dog access to the clothes and your garage. Search for your dog in the immediate area for places he may be hiding, including neighbors' open garages, behind bushes, and so on.

Our procedures worked, and within two days, Vicki called to tell me her dog made it home and was fine. What a relief! Now that the drama of nearly losing another dog was over, I told Vicki it was time to set up a few procedures in her home so this situation never occurred again.

I encouraged Vicki to require her roommate to make some changes. First, her roommate would no longer leave the house through the front door. Second, her roommate would exit the house through the garage. In doing so, she opens and closes the door from the house to the garage, makes sure the dog is not in the garage with her, and only then opens the garage door to go to her car.

Pretend, for a moment, that you are caring for a human toddler. These tiny tikes are mobile, agile, and energetic, but also clueless about safety and security. You are responsible for everything associated with their health, wellness, and safety. You're the parent in charge of what happens to them until they become an adult. Guess what: once you have a pet, you are essentially in charge of a toddler for the duration of his or her life. In the home, my team and I apply simple protocols and use proven tools to ensure pets are both safe and healthy. Now I want to share them with you.

Exits & Entrance Blocks

- **Doors:** If you have a "runner," a dog or cat that shoots out the front door at every possible opportunity, place a block at the front door. This can be a retractable block like the Bow Wow Barrier or a folding security gate.

Service Providers

- **Gate/Crate:** Don't rely on service providers (a plumber for example) to make sure your pets are secure in the house when they come and go. It's your dog, so it is your responsibility. Every month we will hear multiple pleas from parents asking for help to find their dog that got out of the backyard when their landscaper (or pool guy) opened the gate to mow their lawn or clean their pool. Gate or crate your dog so they can't get out while service providers are working in/around your home.
- **Contractual Help:** If you have contracts with a maid service or HVAC provider who automatically arrives at your home on a regular basis, request the same representatives who know you have pets inside your home. In doing so, you have people coming and going who are more aware of how to safely enter and leave your home without letting your pets escape.

Line of Sight Prep

It's a lot easier to protect your beloved pets when you can see them. One of the simplest safety measures in your home is to configure your living space to ensure your dog is always in your line of sight.

- **Doors:** Keep all doors to extra rooms closed: bedrooms, bathrooms, utility rooms... This forces your pet to stay in your primary family spaces (living room/dining area or maybe your home office) where they remain in your line of sight. Further, this simple step also prevents your dogs from getting into bathrooms where they can access medicine cabinets and children's rooms where they can pick up and swallow tiny toys, socks, etc.

Toddler-Proofing

- **Furniture:** Look behind and under all furniture to make sure there are no small items available for a dog to swallow. When you clean house, or a maid service cleans your home, be sure to clean under all furniture every time to prevent easy-to-swallow items from collecting there.
- **Anchor:** Be sure to anchor tall, heavy furniture to walls so they can't fall over on your pets.
- **Cabinets:** Lock all cabinets where dogs can access chemicals or cleaners.
  - Dreambaby® has a line of easy-to-use cabinet locks, but bungee cords will work too.
- **Counters:** Many dogs are large enough to become stellar "counter surfers." Counter surfers are dogs tall enough to stand up on their hind legs and reach via their tongue and front paws, anything they deem edible that is sitting on your counter. Accessing the top of kitchen and bathroom counters provides your pets with a buffet of items to ingest: plastic Zip Lock bags they can choke on, grapes sitting in a bowl (toxic for dogs), your anti-inflammatory meds (dangerous for dogs), knives that can put out an eye, the list goes on.
- **Stove:** Don't forget to turn handles of pots and pans on the stove away from the edge of your counter.

- **Toys:** Make sure all small human toys are picked up. Throw away any dog toys that are falling apart to avoid the chance your dog will swallow a piece or ingest the stuffing from a plush toy.
- **Cords:** Young dogs will often chew or pull on electrical cords. Cover them with cord covers or block them with furniture. Block dogs from getting under beds and sofas where they can access cords. This can be done with a variety of products, including the Upstone® Gap Bumper and the BowerBird Under the Bed Dog Blocker, for example. Use pull-away power cords that automatically unplug from appliances so your dog can't pull appliances off counters and onto their heads.
- **Trash:** Either place trash cans where they can't be reached or use trash cans with a strong seal. Trash cans in the kitchen, filled with tempting food smells, and in the bathroom are especially *attractive* to your dog. However, the smelly temptations inside could be rancid food or old pharmaceutical drugs you've discarded.

Water/Food

- **Bowls:** Use stainless steel bowls. It is easier to clean/disinfect and unbreakable.
  - **Note:** stainless steel bowls with skid-proof bottoms are best. Wash and thoroughly rinse bowls every day. Ceramic bowls are too easy to break. Plastic bowls are easy for dogs to chew up (creating pieces to swallow) and prone to scratches. Scratches produce indentions where bacteria can build up, making it difficult to keep plastic bowls sterile.
- **Food:** If you have more than one dog, feed them in separate areas. This avoids the possibility that your dogs will become food aggressive because they are afraid the other dog will eat their food. It also ensures dogs don't eat food that could upset their stomach.
- **Chews:** I can't recommend any type of animal hide chews. They are too difficult for dogs to digest. Some non-hide chews can be given to your dog to occupy their time or to keep their teeth clean. However, you should *always* store these away when you are not at home with your pet.

Pet Care Security

At Creature Concierge, we tell our pet parents, "Your pet is only as safe as your home." Security of your home, when you're not at home, must be a top priority if your pet is to remain safe in your absence.

Review the security measures used by your pet care professionals and extended family if they care for your pet when you're away. These measures are always important, but especially so during popular traveling holidays when opportunists are looking for a chance to break into a home. Creature Concierge has stringent security protocols. I've listed some below. These protocols are designed to ensure your home (and in turn, your pets) are safe at all times, because it *appears* someone is home at all times. To that end, consider these guidelines:

- **Signs/Car Wraps:** Pet service providers should remove all company identification on vehicles, clothes, and hats. This brings attention to anyone watching the home that family members are gone.
- **Keys:** No client names or addresses are written on key fobs. Should a key be lost and picked up by another person outside the family, no one can tie that key to a specific home.
- **Mail:** Packages on the doorstep, mail, and newspapers in the yard should be picked up daily and placed inside the home. Delivery stickers and solicitation door hangers need to be removed daily.
- **Trash:** Waste containers (trash and recycling) should be taken out to the curb on the appropriate day and returned to their storage site at the end of that day. This should be done even if they are empty.
- **Neighbors:** Alert immediate neighbors, who you know well, when you will be out of town and inform them which vehicles will be at the house. For example, a pet care specialist's car, pool service provider's truck. Make sure your pet sitter knows which neighbors have been informed of their arrival.
- **Routines:** Lights, shutters, blinds, and curtains should all be adjusted at appropriate times to mirror the homeowners' typical schedules and routine habits.

- **Holidays:** Christmas holiday lights that are not on automated timers should be turned off and on to indicate the homeowner is in town.
- **Service Providers:** Carry a list of any additional service providers' company names that will be in and/or around the home when the parents are absent. Ask the pet sitter and/or neighbors to report if they see any service vehicles or uniformed workers around the home that are not on the list.
- **Weather:** Be aware of daily weather forecasts alerting homeowners of destructive hail, flooding, hurricanes, tornados, snow storms, etc. that could damage the home and harm the pets. See Chapter 7 on Preparing for Disasters for more weather-disaster preparation details.

CHAPTER 16

Prevent Accidents Outdoors

Your yard is simply an extension of your home and, in turn, another place to make pets safe. By acting more defensively when outdoors, you can prevent accidents and injuries that lead to medical emergency care for your pet or worse, their loss. This chapter of your guide is designed to teach you the most important safety measures outdoors in your yard and neighborhood.

Prevent Accidents in Your Backyard

- **Gates:** Make sure all gates have a lock on them. The lock may be a simple carabiner looped through the gate's lock holes to ensure a kid doesn't inadvertently opens the gate.
- **Providers:** Bring dogs in the house or gate/crate in a sheltered area when service providers are working in your yard. Landscaper equipment can fling debris and harm a dog's eyes. After pool and lawn service providers complete their work in your backyard, check your fence gates to make sure they are securely closed and locked prior to letting your dogs outside again.
- **Insecticides:** In Chapter 19 of this guide, I alert parents to common things in the yard/around the home that can poison your pet. In this section, my focus will be on insecticides. Fertilizers, rodent trap bait, and ant poison are just a few of the items we use around our pets without thinking of the harm they can cause if ingested. If you use an exterminator, find out what they use and discuss organic alternatives. Make sure you know dry times and any other safety measures that should be considered before you allow your dog around these products. Never let your dog chew or eat grass during a walk. You never

know if it has been sprayed with weed killer or some other type of insecticide.
- **Doggie Doors:** Although convenient for humans and dogs, experience has shown us that doggie doors can be a challenge to your dog's safety. Due to the prevalence of predators (bobcats, coyotes...) that can jump over backyard fences, we don't recommend doggie doors at all for small dogs. At the least, place the block over your doggie door from nightfall until sunrise so you can be sure to always have a human with your dog when they go outside in the early dawn, at dusk or anytime at night.
- **Fencing:** Check the height of your fence. There are certain mid-sized breed dogs (as small as twenty pounds) and many large dogs that can easily scale fences up to five feet in height. Is your fence height suitable for your dog as a small puppy *and* as a grown dog? If not, take immediate action to prevent your dog from getting out of your yard. Here are a few ideas to help:
  - **Neuter:** If you have a male dog and he is not neutered, schedule a neutering procedure. Intact males have a high propensity to roam, fight, and chronically escape from a home. I brought one intact male back to his parents five times one summer, as he would escape any way possible to find a female. The owners of this dog eventually lost their dog permanently.
  - **Deterrents:** Some breeds with a genetic disposition to hunt and pursue prey will not be deterred from trying to get out of your backyard. Apply L-Footers, fence extenders, or cat netting at the top of your fence. Plant a row of thick shrubs or install a lower inner fence to make it impossible for your dog to get the running start it takes to jump over the top. Shrubs, if you have a chain link fence, may be the best alternative as they also block your dog's view from seeing the squirrels, dogs, rabbits, and lizards that motivate them to jump the fence. PVC pipes that roll on top of the fence can make it very difficult for a dog to get a grip and jump over.
  - **Boosters:** Remove items that can be used by your dog to climb up a fence or get over a fence. Think twice before you

build structures near your fence line. I know of a tiny terrier that pushed his back feet against a shed next to the backyard chain link fence as he used his front paws to climb up the fence to get to the top. Once a month, walk the fence line to check for any places along the bottom of the fence where your dog could get out (or where your dog is digging to get out).
- o **Distractions:** Puppies and more active dog breeds may try to jump fences because they are bored. Spend quality time helping your dog fight boredom by fetching, playing tug of war, or going through a homemade agility course.
- **Pools:** Having a pool or hot tub is a great perk for humans. Some dogs enjoy these recreational luxuries too. However, they can also be dangerous. Fence off your pool area if you can. If not, be sure to teach your dog how to get to steps in the pool where they can easily get out if they fall in. Don't let your dog around a pool without human supervision.
- **Water/Bird Baths:** Keep fresh, cool water available for your pet at all times. Dehydration is dangerous for your dog. Use an easy-to-clean stainless steel bowl, and clean and refill it daily. Do not leave water bowls full of water outside at night, as it attracts rodents, other wild animals, and mosquitoes that you don't want in or around your yard. Worse, wild animals can contaminate your dog's water. Keep pet-safe mosquito dunks in all water fountains and birdbaths to avoid mosquito infestation. Remember: mosquitoes carry diseases and can also transfer heartworm larva to your dogs.
- **Predators:** Many of our homes are built in areas that are populated with wild animals. Depending on your geographic location, these predators could be bobcats, wolves, coyotes, bears, and mountain lions, to name a few. Some can easily scale a fence. Adult coyotes can jump a five-foot fence. Consider a coyote roller along the top of lower fences to keep coyotes out. Bobcats can scale a twelve-foot fence and are great at climbing trees. Too often we hear of parents losing their pets to these agile, resourceful hunters. Don't underestimate these predators'

willingness to overcome their fear of humans and hunt in broad daylight. We find that many of them, especially in spring and early summer, will hunt at any time in our neighborhoods, looking for food (including our pets) to feed their babies.
- **Waste:** Pick up your dog's waste in the yard and throw it away in a well-sealed container. Letting a yard get littered with dog waste attracts rodents. Rodents carry diseases and can contribute to your dog's exposure to Leptospirosis and other diseases.

Prevent Catastrophes on Your Walks

Go back to the time you were learning to drive. It doesn't matter if it was two years ago or thirty years ago. Driving instructors, parents, and police officials all preach one common lesson: drive defensively. The standard *Safe Practices for Motor Vehicle Operations* defines defensive driving as "driving to save lives, time, and money, in spite of the conditions around you and the actions of others." Good advice. We encourage you to apply the same principle standards when you're "driving" your pet, whether on a leash or in a car. To significantly reduce the chances of losing your dog or your dog getting injured on walks, follow these simple practices.

Gear: Safety begins with what you put on your dog before a walk and the gear you use during a walk. Dog owner gear should include a real flashlight (not a cell phone light) a slip leash, and a collapsible water bowl. For your dog...

- **Collars:** Make sure your dog's collar is securely on your dog with identity/parent contact information tags that are easy to see. Make sure the collar is not too tight. Hook a leash to a harness, not a collar. Leashes attached to collars make it too easy to damage your dog's trachea.
- **Harnesses:** Harnesses are tools, not decorative accouterments. There are some designed to give you more control of your dog, but they should all reduce your chances of losing your dog. Do not be fooled. Many of the harnesses on the market are too easy

for dogs to pull out of, and once they know they can get out of them, they will. Here are a few harnesses to consider:
   - **Sporn® Training Mesh Harness**: Sold at PetSmart®, this harness is strong but lightweight (cooler); it features a comfort band underneath the arms and provides a better fit due to the cinch back and adjustable collar. If your dog insists on wearing a more stylish harness, the design of the harness should mimic the fit-safety measures of the Sporn®.
   - **Buddy Belt©**: These are chic, comfy, secure-fitting leather harnesses. These are better for smaller and some mid-sized dogs. (www.muttropolis.com)
   - **2 Hounds No-Pull©**: For mid-sized to larger dogs that tend to pull, consider switching to a no-pull harness. By hooking up your leash to a loop underneath (at the chest area), the pulling significantly diminishes, making it easier and safer to walk your dog.
     - Tip: If you have a dog that yanks and pulls on the leash, get some help from a trainer to get this behavior in check. Next, remember to never let a dog pull your arm out to its full length. This is not good for your shoulders, and worse, it gives you little control of the dog because you're holding the leash only with your arm. Keep your leash arm in with your elbow close to your body. By doing so, your dog is now pulling against the weight of your back and abdominal muscles (not just your arm) and you have more control.
   - **Gooby ®Perfect Fit X**: This harness is ideal for dogs with a flat-face (Boston Terriers, Pugs, Pekinese) because it won't restrict the neck and chest, which can hinder the breathing of these special dogs.
- **Leashes**: We never recommend a retractable leash. There are many reasons for this, but all parents should know it's simply too easy to get your dog killed using them. If the spring mechanism breaks just when your dog leaps for a squirrel, your dog ends up pulling the cord to its full length off the lawn, off the sidewalk, into the street and in front of an oncoming vehicle. The lock

mechanism fails too easily. Parents get pre-occupied and don't realize their dog is far away where they find (and eat) a dead animal that makes them sick, forcing you to take them to the vet for expensive treatment. Remember, a dog may smell something way before you see it. By the time you see it, it's in their mouth. During walks, I've pulled discarded bones, napkins, bird carcasses, and other disgusting items out of a dog's mouth. In our Pet First Aid/CPR class for parents, we cover more reasons to avoid using a retractable leash. Ideally, use a leather or nylon leash with a latch that you check regularly to make sure it's in perfect working condition. Before you open the door to leave for a walk, put your hand through the end loop of the leash and wrap it around your hand one time. The next time you're caught off guard when your dog lunges for a squirrel or rabbit, instead of losing the leash (and your dog), you will only lose what's wrapped around your hand. This has saved countless owners from losing their dogs.

- **Muzzles:** Most people assume that a dog wearing a muzzle on a walk is doing so because he or she is aggressive. We have dogs in our care that wear muzzles because they will literally eat *anything*. Applying a muzzle to prevent your dog from eating what they shouldn't eat will greatly reduce your chances of incurring expensive vet bills that accompany the removal of those "shouldn't" items.

Stay Unencumbered: Don't use earphones when walking. It's too difficult to hear oncoming vehicles (including those driving out of control at breakneck speeds) and to hear passersby (that may have unruly dogs you want to avoid).

Avoid Distractions: Just as driving while texting is dangerous, walking while using your phone is, too. It's a huge distraction and before you know it, you're engulfed in a lengthy conversation without realizing your dog is standing in a mound of ants or he's drinking gutter water infested with bacteria. If you must take a call on your cell, place your phone on speaker so you can keep your eyes on your dog. Then, make the call quick. A safer alternative, and one we use a lot at Creature Concierge, is to stop and kneel next to your dog during the call.

Environmentally Aware: How many times have you driven through a neighborhood and suddenly a ball rolls into the street in front of you? Without thinking, you hit your brakes because if you see a ball roll into the street, you know there is likely a kid not far away on their way to get it. In much the same way, when I see a fence gate wide open, I start looking for a loose dog that may have gotten out. Some loose dogs are just curious, whereas some are on the hunt. Walk defensively.

Anticipate Surprises: Surprises are inevitable. You don't want to get caught off guard. If you anticipate what could happen, you're more likely to prevent your dog from suffering from most accidents and injuries.

Waste: It's always wiser to have your dog by your side with you leading. If you choose to ignore this advice, be vigilant about surprises of all types, including dog waste that an owner fails to pick up. Dogs are fascinated by the feces of another dog to the point of placing their nose right on it. I always say, "If you (dog owner) are too lazy to pick up your dog's poop, you're likely too lazy to take proper care of your dog." Meaning, the feces may carry diseases (like Giardia) that your dog can catch.

Charging Dogs: Literally, while writing this chapter, I received a text message from a client who read an online neighborhood post about a large dog who broke off his leash and attacked another dog. If you are walking a small dog, and you see a charging dog coming at you, quickly pick up your dog. Avoid making direct eye contact with the charging dog (they may perceive this as aggressive), stay calm, and make yourself look as big as possible. Your confident state and sense of control will often help diffuse their charging energy. If possible, look for something that can serve as a barrier between you and the other dog. Preventing an attack is sometimes possible simply by diffusing an aggressive dog's adrenaline. I've thrown a bowl of water on a dog that was getting too wound up at the dog park. Needless to say, he was shocked and immediately decompressed.

Nature: Spring brings living things to life but not all are good for your dog. Bees in Texas, as they enter the end of their life, begin to hover around the ground and can cause problems for your dog. If you and your dog are hiking in an unfamiliar area, find out what, if any, critters could be dangerous for your dog during the hike. Just weeks ago, there was a news announcement about the giant Asian (Killer) Hornets arriving in Washington State. How do you prevent an attack? Are you prepared to save your dog if he or she is attacked?

Poorly Trained Humans: I have one more warning for my pet lovers. If you see a dog walking a human (i.e., clearly the dog is in control), stay clear of the area. A human walking a dog without the ability to control the dog is an unpleasant surprise just waiting to happen.

CHAPTER 17

Prevent Accidents Offsite

I was driving to a home-service call one day to walk a dog in Carrollton, Texas. I turned south onto Old Denton Road off Hebron. This is a busy intersection with two left-turn lanes that spill onto a three-lane road. Just as I made the turn, the car behind me came around my right so all three lanes on Old Denton were full of cars. Almost simultaneously, we all realized there was a car in the middle lane driving the wrong way. The car was heading directly toward us. I tapped on my horn as did another driver. The car kept coming. I pressed on my horn and everyone stopped their vehicles, hoping the other driver would stop soon. He was two city blocks closer to us when he finally must have heard our horns and looked up. Shocked, he pulled into the shopping center just to our right. The driver, we assume, was texting that entire time since his head was down. I took a deep breath, realized how lucky I was (since I was sandwiched between the other cars in the center lane) and thought about what would have happened to me or a dog in transport had this careless driver not stopped. All the safety equipment in the world, even seatbelt-cinched, crash-proof dog crates, won't fix stupid driving.

Transport

A text takes less than five seconds to send, but your car, moving at fifty-five miles per hour, has already traveled the length of a football field in the same amount of time. That's a sobering 2016 statistic from the National Highway Traffic and Safety Administration (NHTSA). The NHTSA also notes that 52 percent of vehicle accidents occur within five miles of a person's home, and 77 percent of vehicle accidents occur within fifteen miles of the home.

Although the focus of this chapter is on transport equipment and safety practices at other sites, it doesn't hurt to review some driving fundamentals that could save your life and the life of your pet, too.

- Never walk out to the car without securing your dog on a leash first.
- Check your route before heading out so you don't need to use a phone app to find your way.
- Assume every other driver around you is distracted by something.
- Drive like you're the underdog. I got my motorcycle license long ago. Riding a motorcycle around cars makes it abundantly clear how vulnerable you are to any object left in the road and to other cars and drivers that aren't paying attention. I try to drive my car like I'm a vulnerable motorcyclist.
- Before you start your vehicle, check mirrors, windshield wipers (if it's raining), and buckle up. The NHTSA notes that seatbelts save 13,000 lives every year.
- Don't leave your dog in the vehicle. Aside from the danger that they could be stolen, the condition inside your vehicle can jeopardize your dog's life when it is extremely cold or extremely hot. On an 85-degree day, even with your windows slightly down, the temperature in your car can reach 104 degrees in *ten minutes*. Thirty minutes later, your dog is in a 119-degree vehicle suffering from irreversible organ damage that can lead to death.

Following these common-sense guidelines and using the right transport equipment will prevent injuries while transporting your creature kids to daycare/boarding facilities, dog parks, groomers, or veterinarian visits.

Crate Equipment

Transporting your dog in a crate securely anchored in your car maximizes safety for you and your dog. In some states, it's against the law to transport an unsecured pet. Dogs left to run around in the vehicle are more vulnerable; they are also a major diversion to you. CarRentals.com released a study revealing how unsecured dogs in the car became a distraction. Forty-one percent climb in the owner's lap, 27 percent nudge their drivers for attention, 11 percent block the passenger side window during the drive, 10 percent get sick, 9 percent stand on the center console, 2 percent step on the gear shift. You can now see the value of crating your dog while traveling.

Unfortunately all crates are not created equal, nor are all the same crates (or harnesses) best for every size dog. The Center for Pet Safety (CPS) was established in 2011 to develop performance standards and test protocols for pet safety devices. CPS revealed the majority of crates are not safe. In addition to the type of crate you choose, the location of where you place the crate in your vehicle is equally important. Avoid crumple zones and passenger seats (where your dog could get hurt from an airbag) and use a crate that performs well in a crashworthiness test.

Size matters! Choose the crate size suitable for your dog. For length, measure your dog from the neck where the collar sits to the tail and then a few inches further. For height, measure from the top of your dog's shoulders to the ground and then add a few inches.

Small-Sized Dogs

I used to own an estate sale auction business. My team and I would pack up items that didn't sell at an estate sale and resell them via an online auction to raise funds for rescue dogs and cats. I learned quickly that if you carefully wrapped fragile items but left too much space in the box used to transport the items, they were very likely to break during transport. The crate you choose must be the correct size for your dog.

Crates Options: The Sleepypod® Mobile Pet Bed or The Gunner Kennel.

> **Dog Weight Range:** Puppies to dogs weighing up to eighteen pounds. Sleepypods® come in mini and medium. The medium accommodates dogs up to twenty pounds.
>
> **Advantages:** This crate performs well during CPS crashworthiness tests. However, maximum performance of this crate during the test was partially reliant on using a Sleepypod® Handilock device, too. An alternative is the Gen7Pets™ Commuter Carrier. One convenience of this crate is that it is designed to use with your vehicle's existing seatbelt system and in most cases, it is airline approved. Another option is the Petego Forma Frame. This carrier-style crate can be used

in the car and on a plane. Like the Sleepypod®, this carrier has a special latching system, ISOFIX Latch Connection, making it a great CPS crash-tested performer and a safe choice for your pet. A final, albeit more expensive option, is The Gunner Kennel, which passed the CPS crash-study tests with flying colors.

Medium Sized Dogs

Crates should be designed for optimum safety, so wire and soft-sided crates should not be used. Before you leave on any trip, check crate latches and security connectors to make sure they are in full working order.

Crate Options: The Gunner® Kennel or the 4pets© Pro Dog Crate.

Dog Weight Range: Dogs weighing twenty-five to seventy pounds

Advantages: Use the intermediate size or large size, depending on your dog's measurements. The Gunner crate for mid- to large-sized dogs passed the CPS crash study tests with flying colors. Admittedly, they are costly, but I encourage pet owners to weigh both sides of the equation. A one-time cost for a life-saving product that lasts many years versus the cost of emergency hospital veterinary expenses to save your dog that wasn't in a Gunner®. For a more budget-friendly alternative, consider the 4Pets© Pro dog crate. This Swedish-made crate is made of anodized aluminum bars with a reinforced back.

Large and Supersized Dogs

Larger dogs are a challenge during transport not only because few crates on the market proved safe enough for them, but also the inertia created for a large dog during an accident is incredibly dangerous for you and your pet. An eighty-pound dog in a crash in a vehicle traveling only thirty miles per hour will exert approximately 2400 pounds of pressure. Yikes!

Crate Options: The Gunner® Kennel G1, the 4pets© Pro Dog Crate, or the 4x4 North American Variocage

Dog Weight Range: Dogs weighing up to seventy-five to 110 pounds

Advantages: Designed to withstand over 4,000 pounds of force, the Gunner crate features doubled-walled 'rotomolded' plastic. The straps used to secure the crate in your vehicle help with the safety performance of this crate, so make sure to use them. I had to save my money to purchase my Gunner® crate. They are more expensive than most but once you use one, you'll see it's worth every penny. Having said that, the 4pets© Pro Dog Crate is an excellent, less expensive option. It performed well in CPS crash studies and is verifiably certified from the German product inspection agency TUV Sud. For what it's worth, the 4pets ©Proline box happens to be Caesar Milan's transport crate of choice. Finally, not to be outdone, consider the transport safety superstar: the 4 x 4 North American Variocage. This crate was strategically designed and tested to withstand front and rear impact and rollover vehicle crashes. The same company also sells vehicle transport harnesses.

In summary, it's worth taking a little time to research your transport equipment options and then invest in properly secured transport gear that can literally save your dog's life.

Hire the Right Pet Care Professional

Just as it is important to do your due diligence on transport equipment, it is just as important to research the background of the people who transport your pet as well as the staff where you take your dog for daycare and boarding.

Pet Sitters
Most dog walkers are beloved by the dogs they walk because these pet care specialists genuinely love them and want the best for them. This does not, however, make them the best choice. Having a passion for pet care should be a given if you are in the pet services industry. You should expect more. At Creature Concierge, our pet care specialists offer more services for our pets and their parents, but what is also important are the skills, training, experience, education, and certifications of our team. Further, the application of specific processes that ensure measurability, trainability, quality, and consistency when

delivering these services. When selecting a pet care professional, consider the following:

- **Background**

Has this person been vetted? Does the owner of the pet sitting company conduct financial, civil, and criminal background checks on all their pet care employees? Since most pet sitting services include pet transport, their driving records should also be researched to determine if they have multiple driving violations for speeding, driving while intoxicated, etc.

In addition, you will gain some great insights into the person by asking:

- What else has this person done in their career outside of pet care?
- What, if anything, did this person do in the pet care industry before becoming a pet sitter/dog walker (Any work with a dog rescue? A zoo? A local animal shelter? With animal control? A vet office?)
- Why did this person choose this career or job?

- **Experience**

How long has this person been providing pet care services? Direct field experience is critical, so find out how much they have had and what services they've provided in the past.

- **Training/Certification**

There are numerous added value choices for professionals in my business that dog walkers can pursue. Specifically, CPR training, First Aid training, Pet Sitters Certification, Dog Training, Dog Massage Therapy, Pet Nutrition, and Holistic Nutrition, to name a few. Does the staff receive training? If so, on what topics and how often?

- **Education**

Do they have a vet assistant, a vet tech, or veterinarian degree? Do they have a degree in animal sciences, biological science or agricultural science? Don't underestimate the importance of a business background, and degree of some type. This type of background usually yields people that operate a better-running business.

- **Recommendation**

If requested, prospective employees should be able to offer client references. Call them. This is especially important if you didn't hear about this person from a trusted source. Don't rely too much on online ratings and reviews unless you can take into consideration how some people will use this forum to vent about grudges that may not reflect the true nature of the pet sitter's reputation.

- **Flexibility**

What services does the prospect offer? Do they only walk dogs or can they also care for cats, birds, and reptiles? Can they administer medication? Do they provide in-home overnight stays when needed? Do they work early in the morning and late at night? Are they available to provide services Monday through Sunday? What about holidays?

- **Affiliations and Insurance**

Does the company carry liability insurance? Are they a member in good standing with an industry association or group like Pet Sitters International, the National Association of Professional Pet Sitters, or the Professional United Pet Sitters?

Prevent injuries & Illnesses at Daycare/Boarding Facilities

When choosing a private service, daycare/boarding facility, or veterinarian office to care for your dog, get information about the leaders and employees first. Many of the questions used for vetting a pet sitter (on previous pages) apply here too. You want to know about their experience, training, and background-check process. Note: it is also helpful to find out the average tenure of the employees. If turnover is high, there may be some underlying problems with the way the company operates that you consider before using the facility. In addition to getting information on the staff, be sure to ask about security, cleaning, design, food, equipment, and so on.

Security

There are a lot of dogs coming and going in the lobby area. What procedures are set up to make sure they are all healthy and free of contagious viruses? If this is a veterinarian office that provides after-hours boarding, this is especially important. What processes are in place to protect your dog from getting hurt by other dogs that are aggressive? Does the facility provide cameras that parents can use for online viewing?

Cleaning

I was touring a daycare facility one day when I noticed a dog pee, indoors, on the floor. The dutiful employee chaperoning the dogs was quick to clean it up. The problem is the worker was using a common rope-style mop that is very difficult to keep sanitized. Such mops are like a giant germ spreader. What products does the facility use to clean the dogs' toys and equipment? What products do they use to disinfect the dogs' rooms and floors? Are these products pet safe? Does their disinfectant kill bacteria, fungi, and most dog-related viruses like hepatitis B, HIV-1, and Parvovirus, to name a few? What cleaning equipment do they use to apply these cleaners and disinfectants?

Design

Is the flooring of the daycare facility ideal for impact while also being easy to clean and disinfect? Are toys and equipment (indoors and outdoors) well-maintained and designed for safety even for the largest roughhousing dogs? What do they have available for mental stimulation, agility, and exercise? Do they have a pool? If so, how often is the pool cleaned and what products are used? Do they have tire tunnels or tubes to run through? Man-made hills? Bridges? Is the staff standing around or engaged with the dogs as they play?

Food/Water

How are dog meals stored and served to ensure they are kept sanitary? If they eat wet food, is it properly refrigerated? Is clean water available at all times in kennels, play areas, and outside? How often are all the bowls cleaned, and with what?

Supervision

What is the staff-dog ratio? Is there enough staff to supervise and interact with all the dogs in all locations? Is there a staff person in all spaces and rooms at all times? Who is at the facility overnight? What if there is an emergency during the night?

Affiliations

What industry affiliations, if any, does the facility maintain—like the International Association of Professional Dog Daycare Owners (IAPO) or the International Boarding & Pet Services Association (ibpsa.com)? Is the company certified by the Professional Animal Care Certification Council (PACCC)?

Prevent Injuries at Dog Parks

Taking your creature kid to the dog park is like taking a human kid to Disneyland. It's a thrill to play in a large open place while meeting other dogs, too. However, before going, consider the following:

Gates/Fencing

A properly designed dog park will have a dual-entry system. The first area you enter provides a safe, enclosed space to remove your dog's leash prior to taking your dog into the park. Always remove their leash before you go through the second gate. This prevents problems with leash-aggressive dogs. Fencing should be at least five feet tall, but I prefer at least seven-foot-high fences for large dogs. There should be one area for small dogs and one area for large dogs. Security between the two sides is paramount.

The Other Dogs

You probably take excellent care of your dog, but sadly, not all humans do or know how to care for their creature kids. This matters. With a few exceptions, you don't know the other dogs. You don't know if they are vaccinated for diseases and viruses that are easily spread from one dog to the next. Unlike daycare and boarding facilities where pet care specialists require all vaccinations be current, anyone can take their dog to a doggie park.

Sniffing poop is a common behavior for dogs. A dog may just sniff the feces but is just as inclined to put their nose directly on another dog's waste. And yes, some dogs will eat their poop, or another dog's feces, and, in doing so, ingest whatever else is in it. This may include harmful bacteria or a highly contagious parasite like Giardia that is passed from dog to another dog via their feces.

Assuming the dog park you use is filled with happy, healthy dogs, there is something else to keep your eyes on while visiting: the parents. Are they watching their dog? Are they supervising their dog's behavior? Some bury their nose and attention in a book or their cell phone and seldom look up to see what their dog is doing. Keep an eye on your dog to make sure he or she is safe from more aggressive dogs. If you see another dog's negative behavior escalate, get the attention of the parent. If they don't take action, it's better to leave the park.

Maintenance and Resources

Your dog should have a fresh water source available at all times. If you are concerned about your dog using the park's water sources, just carry a water bottle and collapsible bowl with you. Make sure the park has a shade area where your dog can rest and cool off. Check to see that the facility is clean, the poop stations are emptied on a regular basis, and any surfaces (tables/benches) and equipment are cleaned and sanitized. Most dog parks are operated by the city, so call your city resources for any information that is not posted at the site.

Chapter 18

Prevent Poisoning

We headed straight to the veterinary hospital. Paco, a tiny Chihuahua, had ingested several solid Lindt Lindor chocolates. He only weighed eight pounds. Paco was given an immediate injection of apomorphine hydrochloride to force him to throw up. In less than sixty seconds, his little body began to convulse and up came the chocolate (along with the bright, foil wrappers). It appeared he had eaten at least five of the scrumptious chocolate balls—a potentially lethal dose.

Chocolate is highly toxic to dogs and cats. Chocolate contains Theobromine, a naturally occurring stimulant found in the cocoa bean. Once ingested by a dog or cat, it impacts the central nervous system and heart.

Paco was lucky. His pet sitter was washing dishes when he ate the chocolates. She looked up and noticed Lindt wrapper scraps on the floor, found pieces in Paco's mouth and, realizing what had happened, took swift action to remediate the impact on his tiny body. After throwing up all the chocolate and wrappers, Paco made a full recovery.

How did something like this happen? It turns out Paco's sitter had received a large container of the chocolates as a Christmas present from a client. They had placed them in a bowl that they then placed on an end table in their living room. Paco had jumped on the sofa, then jumped on the end table and feasted. It was a simple oversight that could have ended tragically. It was also preventable.

Prevent Poison Hazards

Common Poisons in Your Home

If you've had pets most of your life, you are likely familiar with most household items that are poisonous to your dog. But, just in case, it's good to review the list of foods, products, and medicines that are toxic, even deadly, to your creature kids.

Food

What you may love to eat may be toxic to your pet. Be careful when preparing and serving food to ensure you don't drop food scraps. Even better, gate off your kitchen when you're cooking. In doing so, your dog can't do any "counter surfing" for food that may be toxic to them. Put these items away in a secure pantry or in inaccessible cabinets. It's very important to consider children in regards to food and your dog. Young kids are often sloppy eaters, dropping food on the floor or thinking that sharing with Fido is fun. It's not fun when it's deadly.

Make sure your dog can't access:

- Caffeine
- Candy containing xylitol (like most chewing gum)
- Chocolate
- Grapes
- Macadamia Nuts
- Onions
- Raisins
- Raw Potato
- Walnuts

Products

Humans are big on fighting air pollution outdoors but sadly seldom think of the air pollution inside their home. The US Environmental Protection Agency (EPA) released a report in 2018 highlighting this issue. The EPA noted, "Americans, on average, spend approximately 90 percent of their time indoors, where the concentrations of some pollutants are often two to five times higher than typical outdoor concentrations." Think about the hours your dog or cat spends in the home and the pollutants he or she may be exposed to every day. Some of the pollutant-causing sources are asbestos, carbon monoxide, pressed wood products, lead, nitrogen dioxide, pesticides, radon, second-hand smoke, and household cleaning chemicals. Let's make an effort to *clean house*. Replace pressed wood products, conduct a radon check for your home, request smokers go outside, and introduce non-toxic cleaning products or cleaning materials (like Norwex offers) that eliminate the need for toxic cleaning products.

Bleach:

Chlorine bleach. may be great for whitening socks but it's not good for your dog. Limit its use and keep it safely stored away.

Ammonia:

It is listed in a lot of cleaning products as ammonium hydroxide. There are so many pet-friendly cleaning products on the market now that this should be replaced.

Drain Cleaners:

Use and store carefully.

Dryer Sheets:

The dryer sheets and most liquid fabric softeners contain bengalkonium chloride and cetrimonium bromide that are highly toxic to dogs. Switch to something non-toxic, like Norwex® dryer balls. You can find them on our Creature Concierge website. Just a side note: dryer sheets are also easy for a dog to choke on or even worse, they can get stuck in your dog's GI tract, requiring expensive, emergency surgery to save them.

Floor Cleaners:

Your dog spends hours walking and sleeping on your floors (unless he's like my dog and expects a chic, plush bed). The chemicals in most floor cleaners are extremely noxious to your precious pal. Replace cleaners containing bleach, ammonia, chlorine, phenol alcohol, isopropyl alcohol, and formaldehyde.

Medicine:

My mom is ninety-four years old. She's sharp as a tack, still reads a couple of books a month, and is an incredible baker. The problem is that her hearing is not so good, and she seldom hears when she drops something on the floor. By the time she notices she's dropped a pill, her dog Tinker Toy will have already hoovered it up. Work with the seniors in your care to set up safe medicine practices. My mom now refills her medicine kit in her room or behind the kitchen gate, away from her dog. A thorough floor check before the dogs are allowed out of the kitchen keeps everyone safe.

Marijuana:

The Pet Poison Hotline has experienced an incredible increase in marijuana toxicity cases. The ASPCA Pro reported, "in the first couple of months of 2019, the number of calls related to pets ingesting marijuana jumped 765 percent over the same time last year." Whether for recreational or medicinal use, marijuana is never good for your dog. Dr. Karen Becker reinforced this danger when she warned that dogs are ten times more sensitive to the potent psychoactive cannabinoid in marijuana known as delta-9-tetrahydrocannabinol or THC.

Pain Relievers:

Most of these contain acetaminophen and ibuprofen, which are extremely toxic to dogs.

Pseudoephedrine:

This is a decongestant commonly found in most cold medications. If ingested, a dog may experience a faster heart rate, high blood pressure, excessive panting. If a dog ingests a larger dose, it can be lethal.

Thyroid Hormones:

This contains Synthetic Levothyroxine and desiccated thyroid. An overdose can cause hyperthyroidism in dogs.

Toiletries:

Don't use wipes, shampoos, or conditioners meant for humans on your dog. The pH for humans is different from dogs so these products can irritate a dog's skin and eyes.

Common Poisons in Your Yard

In Chapter 17, I mentioned that you should set your phone alarm to go off each month. This alarm is your reminder to walk your entire fence line and check for holes or areas where your fence is compromised, making it easy for your dog to escape. This is also a perfect time to conduct a parameter check for any products you may have recently used (fertilizers on your lawn, antifreeze in your car, paint thinner on a craft project) but failed to dispose of properly.

Common Poisons Outside or on the Lawn

The products listed below are highly toxic and, unfortunately, are also so common that they are easily found in or around most homes. For ingredients you may not recognize, details are provided so you know what items in or around your home are likely to contain that particular ingredient.

Ant Baits	
Anti-Freeze	
Fertilizer	
Hydrocarbons	(Mineral oil, bath oil, makeup remover, motor oil, waterproofing agents, lotions, etc.)
Insecticides	
Iron	(Vitamins, disposable hand warmers, fertilizers, and prenatal vitamins usually have a higher iron content)
Nitrogen	(Ammonia is high in nitrogen, as well as some indoor plant soil, fertilizers, even coffee grounds)
Phosphorus	(Used in dishwasher and clothing detergents, fertilizers, etc.)
Potassium	(Potassium nitrate is used in sensitive-teeth toothpaste)
Roach Baits	
Rodent Bait	
Slug Poison	

Toxic Garden Flowers:

Next time you work with a landscaper or go to a nursery, take the list of toxic plants below with you to prevent the purchase of plants and flowers that are dangerous to your dog. If you must have these plants in your yard, place them in large pots where your dog can't reach them. You can also gate off parts of your flower garden.

Amaryllis
Asiatic Lily
Azalea
Blood Meal
Bone Meal
Cardboard Palm
Crocus
Cycad Palm
Daffodil
Dumb Cane (also known as Dieffenbachia)
Lilies (Day Lily, Easter Lily, Lily of the Valley, Leopard Lily, Oriental Lily, Peace Lily, Resurrection, Rubrum Lily, Tiger Lily)
Fiddle Leaf Philodendron
Florida Arrowroot
Foxglove
Hyacinth
Japanese Pieris
Jonquil
Kalanchoe
Lady of the Night
Laurel
Mother of Millions
Mountain Laurel
Narcissus
Noon and Night
Oleander
Philodendron
Pothos
Purple Shamrock
Rhododendron

Rhubarb Leaves
Rosebay
Sago Palm
Schefflera
Shamrock
Spring Crocus
Star Fruit (the flowers on the plant)
Sweetheart Vine
Tulip
Umbrella Plant
Yesterday, Today and Tomorrow
Yew
Zamia Palm

Saving Your Pet After Poison Ingestion

Awareness of many of the foods, medicines, products, flowers, plants, and environmental poisons in and around your home is the first step in preventing your pet from getting poisoned. Prevention is always our first goal. However, should your dog ingest something poisonous, take the following steps:

1. Call your veterinarian for help.
2. If it is after hours, call your area veterinarian hospital and then take your dog to the clinic.
3. Call the Animal Poison Control Hotline: (888) 426-4435. This hotline is open 24/7/365 and serviced by experts with extensive experience in helping pet owners deal with virtually any type of poison their dog may have ingested.
    Note: there is a small fee for this service. However, if you are too far from a veterinarian clinic, it is an ideal option (and the fee supports the ASPCA, too).

Before inducing vomiting, (emesis) be sure your veterinarian first knows:

- What your dog ingested. If you don't know but suspect poison, describe details about your dog's condition: vomiting, lethargy, excessive salivating, seizures. You many need to collect a stool and/or a vomit sample for your vet.

- Your dog's breed. If you have a Pug, English Bulldog, Pekingese, or Boston Terrier, often referred to as brachycephalic breeds (smashed-face dogs), it is easy for these breeds to aspirate, so inducing vomiting may not be recommended.
- Provide them with details about the poison. Your veterinarian may not advise emesis of certain products that are easily inhaled into the lungs, where they can cause more damage. So, for example, your vet many not want you to induce vomiting if your dog ingested corrosive products like bleach, lime removal, drain cleaners, alkalis (used in most laundry detergents), ammonia, paint, paint thinner, kerosene, lighter fluid, paint remover, mineral spirits, furniture polish, or gasoline. Batteries are also corrosive—and you may not always consider all the places you use batteries. We had a client with a dog that destroyed a mechanical toy. I had them gather all the pieces and send photos to me. Where was the battery? It was the kind of toy that had a tiny watch battery inside it. I asked them to give me the name of the toy. After asking Mr. Google about the manufacturer, I was able to track down a company phone number and talk to their safety department. I explained what happened. They told me where to find the battery and the parents looked through the plastic pieces to (thankfully) find the battery sealed behind a plastic panel.

Do not induce vomiting if:

- Your dog swallowed a sharp object. Like acid based poisons, the object may do more damage coming up.
- Your dog is unconscious.

Should the veterinarian instruct you to induce vomiting, you can use this common, at-home hydrogen peroxide formula. Specifically:

- **First,** if it has been two hours since your dog has last eaten, you might give him a little food as this will likely make it easier for him to vomit.
- Prepare one teaspoon of hydrogen peroxide per five pounds of your dog's weight.

Note: the maximum dose is three tablespoons for dogs weighing more than forty-five pounds.
- Place the solution in a syringe to administer to your dog. If you don't have a syringe, you can use a turkey baster from your kitchen. Do not place the syringe in the center of the mouth, as this often triggers a gagging reflex. Place the syringe on the side and back of the mouth and slowly give them the solution.
- Your dog should begin to vomit shortly. They will usually continue to vomit until all the contents are up. If he doesn't vomit within fifteen minutes, you can give him one more dose.

CHAPTER 19

Prevent Dental Disease

I was recently discussing dental care with the mother who owned a small dog. Her dog's breath was really bad and a cursory view of his teeth made it clear he needed to have them cleaned. I suspected he would need antibiotics (for infection) and some extractions, too. I encouraged her to discuss dental surgery with her vet. It turns out his teeth were in terrible condition and he needed surgery for a dental cleaning and multiple extractions. My team and I at Creature Concierge see this situation far too often.

The American Veterinary Medical Association (AVMA) noted that 63 percent of pet owners consider their pets to be family members, but only one-third of pet owners provide basic dental care for their pet. The AVMA issued a more alarming statistic reflective of pet owners neglecting the health of their pet's teeth and gums. Eighty percent of dogs and 70 percent of cats show signs of oral disease by the age of three. Think of the expense of trying to save your dog's teeth rather than preventing dental decay in the first place. Owners of insured pets spent $7.2 million in 2009 (on dental treatments) and $11.2 million in 2013 on pet dental conditions.

Click on this quiz to determine how knowledgeable you are about pet dental health. Take the American Veterinary Medical Association (AVMA).

Why is dental health so important? First, you avoid the expense of dental surgery and extractions due to dental neglect. Two, having healthy teeth and gums can also save your pet's life. Dental disease, left unattended, can lead to heart disease.

How To Prevent Oral Disease?

Brush Your Dog's Teeth

We recommend using a toothbrush made for humans. Use a toddler's toothbrush for smaller dogs, an adult toothbrush for large dogs. Toothbrushes made for humans are easier to grip and the bristles are much softer than most toothbrushes made for dogs. Do not use human toothpaste. Many contain Xylitol or Potassium Nitrate, both of which are toxic for dogs. Use a veterinarian-approved dog toothpaste like Petsmile® or Virbac's® CET Toothpaste. One of my favorites: Petz Life Gel. There are also organic toothpastes available (Kissable™ All Natural pet toothpaste). If you prefer US-made products, try Vet's Best® dental gel toothpaste. Use downtime with your pet (watching TV, sitting at the park) to regularly touch your dog's teeth and rub your cat's gums with your (clean) fingers. This keeps them accustomed to having human fingers in their mouth and will make it easier for your pet to have their teeth cleaned. Without brushing, the downward spiral that leads to periodontal disease begins with:

Plaque: Contains bacteria, food particles, saliva, and epithelial cells. If untreated, it hardens to form tartar.

Tartar: That thin film of organic matter that sticks to the teeth. If you don't brush your dog's teeth to remove tartar, it promotes plaque build up, irritating the gums and causing inflammation, which can lead to gum disease.

Gingivitis: Once gum disease, caused from the buildup of tartar around the gum line, progresses, your pet has gingivitis.

Periodontitis: Occurs when pockets between the gums and teeth become infected with bacteria.

Get an Annual Dental Checkup for Your Dog

It's ironic that we love our pets so much, but still tend to care for them as a reactive gesture (after they get sick) rather than a preventative one (before they get sick). According to the AVMA, most parents did not provide preventative care. Oral health for dogs is no different than it is for humans: preventative measures keep teeth and gums healthy. Every year your dog should get a comprehensive wellness checkup. Make sure this checkup includes a dental health review. Not only do you want to make sure your pet has overall dental health, it is also important to look for baby teeth that never fell out, fractured teeth, bone infections, and oral tumors, to name a few. If your pet has more complicated or extensive dental issues, consider seeing a veterinary dentist/oral surgeon.

Have Your Dog's Teeth Cleaned Annually

Most pet owners don't realize that their dog can get their teeth cleaned in a similar way that humans have their teeth cleaned. Referred to as Non-Anesthetic Dental Scaling, it is a process of cleaning your dog's teeth without anesthesia. This is a wonderful method for maintaining the health of your dog's teeth. It is also one of the dental health techniques available for dogs that may have a high-risk medical condition that prevents them from going under anesthesia.

Serve Your Dog A Healthy Diet

What your dog eats makes a significant difference in their dental health and, in turn, the smell of their breath. See the Nutrition section of this guide for details about healthier food options and low sugar/low fat/low calorie treats that contribute to healthy teeth and gums.

Give Your Dog Recreational Chews

As opposed to treats that are quickly consumed, the right chew will provide hours of slow chewing motions that help keep your dog's teeth free of plaque. Avoid dental chews that are too hard. It's easy for your dog to fracture a tooth. Purchase chews that are made in America and are a good fit for your dog. For example, it can be too easy for your dog to choke on a chew because it is too small. Work with your veterinarian to determine the best (and safest) chew for your dog.

Schedule Dental Surgery (if necessary)

What are the tell-tale signs that your dog has dental disease? The most common signs of dental disease are gums that bleed when you brush their teeth, chronic bad breath, red/inflamed gums and yellowing teeth. You may also notice your dog or cat is having difficulty chewing hard food. Schedule a veterinarian appointment to determine if these issues require surgery. If so, be sure to:

- **Do Bloodwork**: Bloodwork before surgery can help identify an underlying infection that could slow your dog's recovery after surgery. Worse, the bacteria from infected gums can travel through the bloodstream to the heart and infect the heart. In some cases, your veterinarian may have your pet take antibiotics for an infection before the dental surgery.
- **Get X-rays:** I have parents ask me all the time if this is necessary. They often feel their veterinarian is just trying to make more money on another service. Not so. I remind all parents that you want to put your dog under anesthesia only if necessary and as few times as possible. To that end, X-rays expose hidden dental problems under the gum line. Avoid having to put your dog under anesthesia eleven months down the road (again) due to a dental emergency you could have seen coming by taking x-rays ahead of time.

CHAPTER 20

Prevent Obesity

It's a sad statistic, but one all pet parents should be aware of: a 2018 Association for Pet Obesity Prevention (APOP) report revealed over half of our pets (55.8 percent of adult dogs and 59.5 percent of cats) in the US are obese. This equates to 50 million dogs and 56 million cats in the pet population.

Prevent Pet Obesity

Why do pet parents need to help their creature kids maintain a healthy weight? First, overweight pets are not living the quality life they deserve. They may be happy, but they are often suffering. Their energy is minimized, their joints hurt, and the joy they used to have for playing or going on walks is diminished. Further, an obese dog is a walking time bomb for terrible, expensive health problems.

Excessive weight leads to osteoarthritis, high blood pressure, kidney disease, insulin resistance, Type 2 diabetes, heart and respiratory disease, ligament injury and a decreased life expectancy of up to 2.5 years. Why, when you love them so much, would you fail to help your beloved pet maintain a healthy weight and avoid all these health-compromising conditions?

Second, some pet parents don't contribute to their pet's healthy weight because they don't realize their pet is overweight. An APOP report noted that 22 percent of dog owners and 15 percent of cat owners said their pet's weight was normal when their pet was actually overweight or even obese. They are not in denial; they genuinely think their pet is at a healthy weight.

There is a third, more disconcerting reason why some pet owners fail to help their pets maintain a healthy weight: many parents get defensive when they are told their pet is overweight. What parent wants to be told their child is obese? I remember in my early corporate days when I was producing special events for Joske's (a retail chain), fitness was the rage at the time due to super personalities like Richard Simmons. We flew Mr. Simmons in to present fitness and health seminars after fitness fashion shows. After one of these presentations, I was escorting Simmons to the limo to go to the next store when a little boy walked up to him. He looked to be about nine years of age. Simmons knelt down to talk to the boy.

"How can I help you?" Simmons asked the boy.

"I wanted to see your show but we didn't make it on time," the boy responded.

The boy was visibly overweight and he communicated to Simmons that he had come to get help to lose weight. Simmons knelt down to the little boy's level and told him he would be glad to help, but first he wanted to talk to his father. It should be noted that the father was a rough-looking, tall (about 6'2" to 6'4") cowboy that towered over his boy and Simmons. Richard was a larger-than-life guy, but he wasn't big. Standing at his full 5'7" height, Richard looked the father right in the eye and said, "You know this is your fault, right?" I took a deep breath and prayed the guy didn't knock Simmons right across the head.

There was a brief, quiet moment and then the father said, "Yes, I know." They talked and set up a way for the boy to work with Simmons to lose the weight.

It's hard for veterinarians, even the most diplomatic ones, to tell parents their pet is obese and needs to lose weight. You would be surprised how many times this angers parents, even offends them so much that they leave that veterinarian practice. How can you get help for your pet if you only listen to what you want to hear?

If you own a pet, you're a parent. You're responsible for their health, happiness, and well-being for their entire life. This means you are also responsible for making sure your pet maintains a healthy weight. If you can own that, you can learn how to fix it.

In summary, even the most caring, seasoned veterinarians in the US have little nutritional training during their college years or thereafter. The lack of extensive diet and nutritional education for our veterinarians makes it more difficult for parents to learn how to help their pets eat the right food that ensures a healthy weight. Most parents have no idea what is in common dog food and couldn't tell you how it directly contributes to weight gain or health problems. Is it possible that one of these reasons is preventing you from helping your dog maintain a healthy weight?

How Should My Pet Look?

It is common for veterinarians to use a Standardized Body Condition Score (BCS) to determine the health level of a dog's weight. Before talking to your veterinarian again, download a Body Condition System chart. The chart provides a visual definition of how your dog receives a number based on an evaluation of fat at certain locations on their body. Some scoring charts run on a 1–5 scale, whereas other veterinarian practices use a 1–9 scale. A dog with a 1/9 score would be emaciated where as a dog with a 9/9 score would be morbidly obese. If your dog has an ideal weight, the ribs will not be visible but only slightly covered by muscle, and the waist will be discernible when you look over your dog.

Tip: If you own a dog with very thick fur, it is best to feel the muscle over the ribs.

Initiate a conversation with your veterinarian about your dog's weight. Invite their honest feedback and get your dog's Body Condition Score today.

Prevent Pet Obesity

Take action to prevent your pet from getting overweight. If your pet is already overweight, step up your parenting skills and get your pet's weight back to a healthy level.

Get Active

Make sure you set up a plan of action with your veterinarian. Introduce more *activity* into your dog's schedule. This can come in a multitude of ways:

- Walk: it's good for you and your pet.
- Swim: If you are blessed to live around a lake or have a pool at home, consider the benefits of having your dog swim with you. It's a fun, calorie-burning activity that avoids placing undue stress on their joints.
- Introduce interactive toys into your pet's daily routine to engage your dogs in physical activity that is also mentally stimulating. This can be as simple as running an automated laser light for them to chase to teaching them how to play balloon volleyball.
- Food Fun: purchase a kibble ball. One of my favorites, made by Omega, has the durability to hold up for long-term use. Instead of serving your dog's kibble in a bowl, measure out the proper quantity and pour it all into the Omega. There is a lip inside the ball that forces your dog to vigorously push, roll, and rotate the ball in order to get kibble out. It's a great activity for their body and their mind.

For a list of fun, inventive methods to keep your dog's mind and body engaged and healthy, download a free copy of The Best Doggie Distractions.

Make Smart Food-Related Decisions

Schedule:

You are caring for a dog, not a cow. Cows graze; your dog should not graze. Serve meals at designated times of the day versus letting your pet eat all day. Grazing can sometimes lead to dogs feeling like they have to guard their food. This can sometimes lead to food aggression. Another reason to avoid grazing is that we encourage feeding dogs fresh, raw, or dehydrated raw food. Fresh food should not be sitting out all day. (See Chapter 23 for food recommendation details.)

Measure:

Serving the right food (healthy and low fat) is not enough. Every meal should be measured to ensure your pet is getting the right quantity of food. Keep a measuring cup with your dog and cat's food. The right food served in the wrong quantity can still contribute to obesity, diabetes, and pancreatitis. If you need help determining how much your dog should eat, consider using the Merrick food calculator.

Treats:

Every treat is a contributor to the daily calories your pet is getting. Be stingy with them. Serve them like rewards, not another meal. Switch to natural foods for treats. Not only does this make it easier to reward your dog and cat with healthy food, it will also reduce the calories they are ingesting every day. For dogs, this might be green beans, carrots, or broccoli; for cats, this might be Bonito flakes. One of the easiest 'treats' to serve your dog or cat is their food. If your pet eats a cup of food for breakfast, skim some food off the top of each meal and use it for treat time. This may not be a big deal to you but for pets that *love* food, it's a very big deal. Tip: see the Nutrition section of this guide to see what is inside some commercial pet treats that may be contributing to your pet's weight problems.

Meals:

What you feed your dog matters. Take the time to work with your veterinarian and, if necessary, a pet nutritionist to determine the best meal plan that will help your pet lose weight and/or maintain a healthy weight. See the nutrition section of this guide for more helpful information and tips. Right food, right quantity: calculate the amount of calories to feed your creature kid.

Habits:

Too many dogs eat too fast. Aside from the fact that this makes it easy for them to choke to death, rushed eating can create a condition called bloat. Bloat (also known as gastric dilatation-volvulus) occurs when a dog swallows a lot of air as he eats. This can cause the stomach to expand and can be life threatening. Eating fast also reduces your dog's ability to digest and absorb the nutrients in the food, so they are full but always hungry. Slow your dog down when eating by serving their food in a slow bowl suited for his size and breed. One of my favorite slow bowls, designed by Outward Hound®, forces dogs to use their tongue to retrieve food between crevices and corners which slows their eating.

STEP FOUR

NUTRITION

CHAPTER 21

The Big Three

My job, caring for people's pets, has many benefits. It is the most rewarding work I've ever experienced, it is joyous, and it has been exceptionally enlightening. One of the advantages my team and I have is that we get to spend a lot of quality time with many of our (pet) clients. We see them more than their groomer and their veterinarian. Our collective time and observations have enabled us to notice, oftentimes before anyone else, if a dog is struggling with intermittent (and excessive) gas, nausea, constipation, diarrhea, and vomiting. The worst cases have watery, bloody stools, lethargy, colitis, and poor dental health. Despite ruling out bacterial infections, viruses, and parasites, many pets we see are exhibiting these symptoms. Further, too many of our beloved pets are suffering from chronic digestive issues and pancreatitis, as well as life-threatening conditions like obesity, diabetes, and cancer.

I want to share some sobering statistics with you. If you read Chapter 20, you now know that nearly 56 percent of our dogs and almost 60 percent of our cats are obese. The Association for Pet Obesity Prevention (APOP) defines obesity as an animal weighing 30 percent or more above their ideal body weight. Obesity is one contributor to pancreatitis and diabetes.

Diabetes is also on the increase. A 2016 Pet Health Report of a comprehensive Banfield Study (with 2.5 million dogs and 500,000 cats) noted a rise in diabetes of nearly 80 percent in dogs and 18 percent in cats over a ten-year period. One in every 300 dogs and one in every 230 cats will develop diabetes. A third, and equally frightening statistic is the increase in cancer. Fifty years ago, cancer occurred in about one in 100 dogs. Today, dogs have the highest rate of cancer of any mammal on the planet. One in 1.65 dogs will succumb to cancer, as well will one in three cats. Twenty percent of pets over five years old die of cancer; 40 percent of pets over ten years of age die of cancer.

Why? My first thought was genetics, but an A&M University study indicates otherwise. The study revealed, "Your dog is four times more likely to get breast cancer than you are, eight times more likely to get bone cancer than you are, and up to thirty-five times more likely to get skin cancer than you are." However, according to a 2008 Springer study published on PubMed, only five to ten percent of all cancer cases can be attributed to genetic defects.

There seems to be a common denominator behind many of the health issues that our cats and dogs are suffering from: chemicals. This includes chemicals in their food and in their environment. Are the foods we are feeding our pets too high in fat? Is the food we give them lacking critical nutritional components? Is it filled with harmful ingredients, or is it deficient in digestive enzymes? What external toxins, if any, are our pets exposed to that would give so many of them such drastic health problems? This segment of this book is to help you be more aware of what's in most of the commercial food many pet owners give their pet, how it can impact your pet's health and, if need be, how to make smarter decisions about what you feed your pets.

CHAPTER 22

A Mini Guide on Common Commercial Pet Foods

My dog Nokona had chronic stomach issues. I could often hear the gurgling noise emitting from his stomach. He ate grass all the time and his stool was hard as a brick, making it difficult for him to go to the bathroom. I've learned that dogs will sometimes eat grass as a way of settling an upset stomach. Nokona was eating a *high-quality* commercial kibble, but the stomach noises and lethargy continued. Nothing improved, but his veterinarian checkups didn't reveal any underlying issues (parasites, bacterial infection). I switched to another variety of kibble but Nokona struggled with the same symptoms with the addition of one more: his breath became horrible. His teeth were cleaned annually (and I brushed his teeth), but nothing helped. The vet tech that cleaned his teeth was pleased with the health of his teeth and gums and suspected his bad breath was coming from his gut. I did too.

Finally, I decided to try something other than kibble. I started feeding Nokona dehydrated food with some raw lamb. Although his breath did not improve, his stool became healthier (firm, but no longer hard like a brick). He still ate grass, but not nearly as often. I tried probiotics but did not see much improvement. I wondered, *does Nokona have a food intolerance?*

A food intolerance occurs when a dog or cat struggles to digest a specific ingredient or multiple ingredients. I called Texas A&M for help and they referred me to the University of Tennessee's animal nutrition program. This program enables parents to send in their dog's food history, along with other information, to university nutritionists. The outcomes are very helpful: they can determine what nutrients your dog needs, what vitamins they need more of, formulate a custom diet for your dog, and much more.

Before using the University of Tennessee's services, I decided to slowly transition Nokona to a fresh custom made diet combined with supplements to maximize nutritional value. I noticed some changes almost immediately. He slowly stopped eating grass, the chronic gurgling in his stomach went away, he was profoundly more energetic, and the smell of his stool improved. (I know this last item may sound weird but while a dog's stool should smell, it should not reek.) The biggest surprise I witnessed with Nokona was the change in his breath. It took almost three months, but his horrible breath began to improve, eventually smelling healthy.

Highly processed pet food appeared to play a huge (negative) role in Nokona's overall health. In fact, it seems to contribute to a multitude of health-related problems for many dogs and cats, sometimes leading to obesity, diabetes, colitis, pancreatitis, and cancer. So with all the modern improvements of veterinary medicine, the quality of pet's lives has hardly improved since so many are suffering from these types of conditions.

Are we inadvertently poisoning our pets by feeding them common commercial (dry and wet) food? You can decide this for yourself after you understand what is in the food they are eating.

How is Commercial Kibble Made?

Those cute little bites or pebbles of commercially produced hard food, often referred to as kibble, may not be as healthy for your dog or cat as you think. Consider, before you purchase commercial kibble (for cats and dogs) how kibble is created and what is added to it.

Kibble is produced through a rendering process where slaughterhouse waste (raw meat and meat by-products) unfit for human consumption is cooked at a very high heat to remove moisture and fat to produce a dust-like powder. This extrusion process effects kibble in four major ways. Extrusion:

- Alters the molecular structure of some of the ingredients, especially meat proteins.
  - A 2008 Wageningen University research study published in the Journal of the Science of Food and Agriculture, concluded, "Among the effects of extrusion on pet foods are starch gelatinization, protein denaturation, vitamin loss and inactivation of nutritionally active factors. The denaturation process, which occurs during rendering, causes a protein to lose its shape and in turn its function."
- Virtually destroys the nutritional content in the ingredients.
  - This includes vitamin A, E, and the B-group vitamins which, by the way, are water-soluble and can't be stored. Your dog needs to get B vitamins through their daily diet. This is hard to do when many vitamins are decimated during the extrusion heating process. The previously mentioned 2008 report by the Animal Nutrition Group at the Wageningen University in the Netherlands, noted the extrusion process destroys B-group vitamins, 65 percent of vitamin A, Vitamin E, 4 percent of thiamin, and realized decreased concentration levels of essential fatty acids (omega-3 and omega-6).
- Produces cancer-causing substances.
  - Specifically, when proteins are extruded, carcinogenic heterocyclic amines (HCAs) are created; when starches are extruded, acrylamides are created. The National Cancer Institute defines HCAs as chemicals formed when meat, poultry, or fish is cooked at high temperatures. HCAs are mutagenic, meaning they mutate, causing changes in DNA that may increase a person or pet's risk of cancer. A 2003 study by Knize, Salmon, and Felton, on Mutagenic activity and heterocyclic amine carcinogens in commercial pet foods revealed twenty-four out of twenty-five of the foods tested gave a positive mutagenic response. Knowing this, why would we use the high heat extrusion process to make our dog's food?

- Eliminates the moisture in the food.
    - Typical dry food only has 12 percent moisture, whereas fresh food contains 70 percent. Moisture is needed to prevent organ stress and dysfunction. How many of our dogs are suffering from chronic dehydration and constipation because the food they eat is void of moisture? The dog and cat foods labeled "moist and healthy" are not much better. In fact, one of the most popular moist pouch foods for dogs contains propylene glycol, a preservative that enables the retention of moisture. Propylene Glycol is also closely related to ethylene glycol (antifreeze).

Now that you understand how commercial (kibble) pet food is often produced and the detrimental impact of the extrusion process, it's time to understand what else is in many commercial pet foods. Learning the meaning behind the terms used to describe the ingredients in your dog and cat's food is a good starting point.

What's in Most Commercial Dry (Kibble) & Wet (Canned) Food?

Additives: These are the artificial preservatives included in commercial pet foods to keep them from spoiling to the point that the kibble and canned food can last up to two years or more.

Carrageenan: Derived from certain seaweeds and processed with alkali, this is an emulsifier that keeps food moist, thick, and stable. It can also chronically irritate the digestive system, resulting in intestinal inflammation and leading to colitis, chronic gas, bloating, ulcers, irritable bowel syndrome, irritable bowel disease (IBD), and can lead to cancer. Caution: Nitrates, which increase the chances of developing cancer, are often used in human deli meats for color enhancement and to prolong their shelf life. Not good for us, not good for our pets.

Corn: Corn is an incomplete protein that contains gluten and often, genetically modified organisms, or GMOs. GMOs are created when genes from the DNA of one species are extracted and artificially introduced into the genes of another plant or animal. Corn is the number one crop in America. A 2011 International Service for the Acquisition of

Agribiotech Applications report states 88 percent of our corn crops (and 93 percent of soybean crops) are genetically modified. We are ingesting these GMO-laced crops and so are our pets. GMOs are tied to dogs' allergic reactions, organ toxicity, and digestive problems. Both a 2009 and 2012 study of lab rats that were fed food with GMOs found significant kidney and liver disease, even mammary tumors.

Corn Syrup: This seemingly benign ingredient is actually not safe for your pet to ingest. It is a food syrup (not high fructose) made from the starch in corn. It contains dextrins, dextrose, maltose, and oligosaccharides and is used as a tasty sweetener that shouldn't be in your dog food at all. Healthy, nutritional, fresh food doesn't require sugar to taste good. (Why do you think dogs love our fresh table food so much?) The simple sugars in corn syrup create the Goldilocks Effect: zippy, high-energy spikes up and equally sluggish spikes down. They also increase your pet's chances of obesity and diabetes. Other sweeteners, like Xylitol and Sorbitol are sometimes used. Xylitol is an artificial sweetener that can cause vomiting and loss of coordination. Like Xylitol, Sorbitol is an artificial sweetener that can also create the Goldilocks Effect.

Fillers: Dogs are inherently carnivores, so a species-appropriate meal should be high in healthy protein. To reduce the cost of kibble but keep the protein levels up, manufacturers will add fillers like corn, corn gluten, soy, soybean oil, and certain grains (wheat, barley, flour, rice). This overabundance of cheap fillers diminishes kibble's nutritional levels, degrades the quality and safety of the food, and is also difficult for your dog to digest. A quick review of some of these fillers will make this clear.

Food Dyes: Dyes are added to kibble to create rich chocolate brown tones and bright colors. These are unnecessary chemicals added to make the food look more attractive to humans. The bright colors mimic the fresh vegetables and fruit that are not in the kibble and the brown coating is designed to make the kibble seem more like fresh meat. These dyes are just another chemical for your dog to consume. The caramel color contains cancer agents. Some dyes like Yellow #5, #6, Red Dye 40, and Blue 2 are linked to many dog allergies, hyperactivity, organ damage, and cancer.

Meat By-Products (also known as by-product meal or meat meal): When you see these terms listed as ingredients on the package, consider what they can, and often, include in your pets food. These "by-products" are essentially what is left of an animal after it is slaughtered and all the meat that is processed for human consumption is removed. This slaughterhouse waste can include any internal remains of an animal to serve as rendered low-grade protein, including: beaks, feet, hooves, hides, hair, tails, and snouts. It can also include feathers, brains, undeveloped eggs, parts of tumors, and intestines with remnants of feces in them. Meat meal or bone meal may include roadkill, dead zoo animals, and dead livestock. Many of these ingredients are difficult for dogs and cats to digest (beaks, feet, hooves, hides, tails, and snouts) and in turn, assimilate into the body; some are dangerous for our pets to eat as they can lead to diseased tissue, compromised organs, and tumors.

Preservatives: These are artificial chemicals that enable pet food to sustain a longer shelf life. A list of the most common preservatives in commercial pet food follow along with details of their effects on our pets' health. These effects include making it harder to digest food, constipation, excessive shedding, weight gain, to name a few.

- Butylated hydroxyanisole (BHA): This preservative appears to cause kidney damage and has the compounds that lead to cancer in pets.
- Butylated hydroxytoluene (BHT): This preservative is linked to cancer, both in dogs and humans.
- Ethoxyquin: is not only a preservative, it is also used as a hardening agent to make synthetic rubber, and has even been used in pesticides. Though usually used in minimal amounts, it's cumulative impact on a dog eating the same food every day is why it is a suspected culprit for kidney and liver damage as well as cancer, immune deficiency, leukemia, and blindness.
- Propylene Glycol: This preservative is derived from the same chemical used to produce antifreeze that is highly toxic to dogs, causing Heinz body anemia (when red blood cells are destroyed) and is suspected to cause intestinal blockage in our pets.

Wheat: Although wheat may seem like a harmless ingredient in pet food, only the endosperm of wheat is used in dog food so it has little nutritional value. Instead, it is a highly processed sugar that contributes to more carbohydrate levels in kibble that cause energy swings and weight gain. This in turn contributes to obesity, chronic digestive problems, and allergic reactions.

What is in Your Pet's Treats?

You can now recognize ingredients in your pet's commercially processed food that can be harmful to your creature kids. What about the treats you are feeding your pets? Many treats are packed with ingredients just as harmful. A few examples follow to make my point.

Beggin' Strips®: contain carcinogenic food dyes like Yellow #5 linked to hyperactivity, anxiety, migraines, and cancer (banned in many European countries) and Red Dye 40 linked to hyperactivity, allergies, and immune system cancers.

Milk-Bones™: contain BHAs, cancer-causing agents that produced tumors in lab animals. Some Milk-Bones contain embalming fluid and others contain large quantities of sugar.

Pup Peroni®: contains BHA and Propylene glycol.

I have a little reminder for parents, "The longer the shelf life of the food, the shorter the shelf life of the pet that eats it." Day-after-day, your pet is ingesting chemically and physically altered food ingredients that are not biologically appropriate for them. You don't have to be a veterinarian or a vet nutritionist to understand that a daily menu of highly processed food, packed with chemicals, is no healthier for your pet than it is for you. Processed food contributes to the declining health of our precious pets.

CHAPTER 23

Nutrition - For Health

Now that you are more familiar with commercial pet food ingredients, you probably understand why I am such a passionate proponent of helping you discover more nutritional food options for your "kids." Consider taking the following steps to ensure your pet is eating a healthier diet. Serve your pets food that will contribute to better organ function and greater energy. Optimize their quality of life, and lengthen and enrich their life.

Read Labels

Pay attention to the chemicals used to make your pet's food. Further, don't rely on labels that say they meet AAFCO (Association of American Feed Control Officials) standards. How high are these standards that allow so many artificial chemicals into our pets' food?

Tip: The meaning behind the terms used on pet food labels can be deceptive. Do some homework so you understand what these terms, in the pet food world, actually mean: *premium, 100% nutritious, Complete and Balanced*, to name a few. One of my favorite examples of misleading labels is provided by an FDA.gov comparison review of pet food makers. The example the FDA provides: Food manufacturer "A" touts their first ingredient as meat and the second ingredient as corn, implying the highest content item in their food is meat. Competitor "B" lists corn (meat meal) as their first ingredient and meat second. You're likely to think food A contains more meat than B. However, by the time you remove the water and fat content in both, company B has more animal-source protein from meat meal than the first product had from meat. I just want to remind dog owners that meat *meal* is made from slaughterhouse remnants (not edible for humans) and filled with ingredients that can be toxic to your dog. For more information on pet food labels, go to FDA.gov.

Pay Attention to Recalls

You can sign up to receive pet food recall alerts at www.dogfoodadvisor.com or at www.petfoodindustry.com. You can also go directly to the website page of the company that manufacturers the food you give your dog or cat. Most have an email alert service you can sign up for at no cost. Have you checked to see if the food you give your pet has been recalled? If it has been recalled, why? What other reasons are given for recalling common pet foods?

Would it surprise you to know that petful.com reports the top (most frequently) recalled brands are Blue Buffalo®, Evanger's®, Diamond™ Pet food, Nature's Variety®, Iams™, Pedigree®, Purina®, and Hill's®, Science Diet™? A recent article written by Justin Palmer for I Love Dogs, provided some interesting details about some of these recalls. Specifically, that Hill's® Prescription Science Diet issued food to stores and veterinarians in 2019 with a toxic level of Vitamin D in it, Blue Buffalo® had six recalls between 2010 and 2017, Caesar's® wet food had to recall food in 2016 because there were plastic pieces in it that dog's could choke on, and Canidae® had to recall four products in 2012 because of the presence of Salmonella. Look up the food you're feeding your dog. How many times, if any, has it been recalled and why?

Consider Other Food Options

When I talk to pet owners about food for their creature kids, I encourage them to explore other meal options on the market. I realize everyone has time, budget, and resource constraints, so be creative. Food plays such an important role in your pet's short- and long-term health so take the time to research the best option for your pet, talk to your veterinarian, and consider paying a one-time consultation fee to work with a veterinarian nutritionist. Whenever possible, look for food that provides fresher, nutritionally healthier ingredients.

Raw Food

This is developed to reflect a dog's ancestral diet with a higher percentage of meat and organs, lower carbohydrate content, and healthier fat contents. Raw, unlike kibble, is easier for dogs to digest and improves their coat, digestive tract, skin, stool, and much more. Bacterial contamination is possible, but is rare since a dog's digestive system is shorter and more acidic. Get better informed about raw food for dogs. Dog's Naturally Magazine offers some excellent tutorial styled articles about raw dog food. Brands you might consider: Answers™ Pet Food or Instinct® Raw. Dog's Naturally Magazine offers some excellent tutorial styled articles about raw dog food.

Freeze-Dried Dehydrated Raw Food

More convenient to serve than raw food, as this food is dehydrated so there is no need to freeze it. Dehydration preserves flavor and retains the food's nutritional value until the food is hydrated. Simply rehydrate most of these with warm water and serve a few minutes later. Consider Dr. Marty's™ Nature's Blend, Open Farm®, or Honest Kitchen®. I also recommend considering Dr. Harvey's Dog Food, which makes it extremely easy (and less expensive) to mix dehydrated ingredients with fresh food.

Fresh Food (Homemade)

There are companies that can make the custom meals for you and ship the food to your home. Consider serving fresh food to your dog or cat. You can get veterinarian-developed recipes from The Farmer's Dog™ and purchase the nutrient/vitamin packs you'll need to add to your pet's food. Homemade Food with Nutritional Mixers: Dr. Karen Becker has worked with Merck to develop custom recipes for your pets that you can make at home, plus meal mixer supplements to add to each meal to ensure optimum nutrition. This takes a little prep time once a week but it ensures a much healthier diet and it's not as costly as purchased fresh food.

Fresh Food (Purchased)

If you don't have the time and don't mind spending a little more money, review one of the fresh made pet foods on the market. Some sell both dog and cat food, fresh made and drop shipped to your door once a month. Companies you might consider are: NomNom®, The Farmer's Dog™, JustFoodForDogs®, Ollie®, and Spot & Tango, to name a few. A team of nutritionists and veterinarians passionate about your pet's health develops the best of the fresh food products on the market. They contain no fillers, or preservatives; they only include the meat, vegetables, nutrients, and vitamins vital to your pet's health. Most don't include grains or use ancient grains like quinoa, millet, spelt.

Kibble, but Better:

If you have to serve your pets kibble or commercially produced wet food, consider those with more novel proteins (duck, lamb, bison, turkey) that are less likely to cause allergic reactions or food-intolerance side effects. Avoid kibble with protein sources that often contain GMOs (like corn). Switch to a kibble that uses lower heat and air-drying during the extrusion process; with better quality protein contents. (Examples are Carna4, Nature's Logic, Lotus® or Stella & Chewy®). When possible, serve wet food with human-grade ingredients. Always add a little warm water to kibble to counteract its dry nature, which can contribute to dehydration and constipation in your pets. Finally, enhance the nutritional value of each kibble meal by stirring in healthy toppers, like fresh food, raw food, or freeze-dried raw food.

CHAPTER 24

Knowledge Unleashes Power

Through the years, Creature Concierge became a distinctive resource where parents could get elevated pet care. Specifically, we offer wellness monitoring, care for physically challenged pets and special medical needs pets (who need insulin or anti-seizure meds), support/transport for pets going through chronic disease treatments (for cancer, physical therapy), and hospice care to ensure comfort and love for pets while their parents take a much-needed vacation.

In 2018, I added an online store with more than fifty pet products. Pet lovers can purchase a variety of items personalized with their pet's name and/or photo on it. However, my pride and joy was the addition of Pet Parent IQ. This is where I could focus on educating our pet parents about the latest pet care equipment, new training techniques, medical breakthroughs, nutrition updates, and so much more. I realized that knowledge unleashes the power to discern which options we have are best in any given situation. Knowledge enables us to make more judicious decisions for our dogs that result in better outcomes.

Both my parents were teachers. Learning was integrated into every part of our lives; education was at the core of our life values. Nothing has changed for me. Every day brings new lessons, information, research, data, resources and the support of specialists—all serving up opportunities to learn. Although I wish some of these lessons about pet care had come sooner for me, I treasure what I know now and begin each day with the attitude that I can always raise the bar with more education. All of us, devoted pet owners everywhere, need to be more knowledgeable and more proactively engaged in our pet's care.

At this point, you understand the fundamental responsibility you have to be a pet parent in regards to preparation, attention, prevention, and nutrition. This segment of my book will help you focus on your *continued* education about pet care. These final pages will be the start of your learning library. You will have access to some of the most relevant, enlightening and valuable resources available for pet owners. Use a few minutes every month to explore these tools to continue your pet care education.

Education from Articles & Research

Education from Experts & Specialists

Education from Videos & Webinars

Education from Organizations

Research & Publications

• Pet Health Secrets Most Vets Don't Tell You
A must read! One of the best-written (and informative) parent tutorials on pet food, nutrition and obesity as it relates to your dog or cat's overall health; how it can contribute to cancer. This is a 2018 TTAC Publishing document. Note: There are additional learning resources at the end of this article. You can download the PDF booklet under its original title, TTAPC eBook-final at: www.scribd.com

Dog Food Labels
- What to Look for when reading labels
- A to Z Pet Food: How to Read a Label
- Interpreting Dog Food Labels

Food Content
- Why Limit Starch & Carbs in Your Dog's Food
- Pet Food Ingredient Analyzer
- Rendered Products in Pet Food
- Decoding Pet Food

Food Pets Die For, by Ann N. Martin
- Shocking Facts about Pet Food

Pet Health Network
- Preventative Care for Your Dog

Radon Facts
- Radon Fact Sheet

Experts & Specialists

Your Vet: _____
Make an appointment with your vet today. Leave your dog at home. Pay the office visit fee to ensure time with your veterinarian. Set up a collaborative plan of action to keep your pet healthy.

Dr. Karen Becker
Integrative Pet Care Expert
Dr. Becker's Bites
https://www.drbeckersbites.com

Dr. Pam Montgomery-Fittz
@drpamholisticvet
https://www.latest.facebook.com/drpamholisticvet

Dr. Jean Dodds, DVM
Founder of the Pet Health Foundation (Blog), the creator of the Nutriscan (to test your dog's for food sensitivities.
www.hemopet.org

Blogs, Videos, Webinars & Interactive Tools

- Merck Vet Manual
    Online Alphabetized Veterinary Resource

- Dr Harveys.com
    Online Blog packed with informative tips

- Pet Insurance Quote
    Pet Insurance Comparison Quote Widget

- Dr. Marty Goldstein
    Dog Food Exposed Video

- The Truth About Pet Cancer
    The 7 Part Docu-Series
    Available online or you can purchase the book and CDs

- Radon in Your Home
    Radon Map by state

- American Animal Hospital Association
    Canine Life Stage Calculator

- American Veterinary Medical Association Pet Periodontal Disease Video

Organizations
- AKC.org
- American College of Veterinary Behaviorists (ACVB)
- American College of Veterinary Nutrition
- Canine Journal
- Center for Pet Safety
- Creature Concierge
- Dogs Naturally
- Dogster.com
- Dogtime.com
- Habri.org
- VetStreet.com

For Dog Training
- The Association of Professional Dog Trainers (APDT)
- The Certification Council for Professional Dog Trainers (CCPDT)
- The International Association of Canine Professionals (IACP)
- International Association of Animal Behavior Consultants (IAABC)

CPSIA information can be obtained
at www.ICGtesting.com
Printed in the USA
LVHW010304090721
692196LV00013B/1637